Teaching, Learning, and Assessment Together: The Reflective Classroom

Arthur K. Ellis

EYE ON EDUCATION

EYE ON EDUCATION
6 DEPOT WAY WEST, SUITE 106
LARCHMONT, NY 10538
(914) 833–0551
(914) 833–0761 fax
www.eyeoneducation.com

Library of Congress Cataloging-in-Publication Data

Ellis, Arthur K.
  Teaching, learning, and assessment together: the reflective classroom / by Arthur K. Ellis.
    p.   cm.
  Includes bibliographical references and index.
  ISBN 1-930556-03-9
  1. Activity programs in education. 2. Reflection (Philosophy) I. Title.
LB1027.25 E45 2001
370.11—dc21

00-055153

10 9 8 7 6 5 4 3 2 1

Editorial and production services provided by
Richard H. Adin Freelance Editorial Services
52 Oakwood Blvd., Poughkeepsie, NY 12603-4112
(845-471-3566)

**Data Analysis for Comprehensive
Schoolwide Improvement**
by Victoria Bernhardt

Performance Assessment & Standards-Based Curricula
by Allan Glatthorn with Don Bragaw,
Karen Dawkins, and John Parker

Performance Standards & Authentic Learning
by Allan Glatthorn

**Personalized Instruction:
Changing Classroom Practice**
by James Keefe and John Jenkins

Research on Educational Innovations, 2nd ed.
by Arthur Ellis and Jeffrey Fouts

**Staff Development: Practices that
Promote Leadership in Learning Communities**
by Sally Zepeda

The Paideia Classroom
by Terry Roberts with Laura Billings

ABOUT THE AUTHOR

Arthur K. Ellis, a former teacher, is Professor of Education and Director of the International Center for Curriculum Studies at Seattle Pacific University. He previously was Professor of Education at the University of Minnesota. His public school teaching experience was in Oregon and Washington. Dr. Ellis is the author or coauthor of 18 published books and numerous journal articles. He consults to school systems in the United States and is involved in a wide range of professional activities in Russia, China, Spain, and other countries. He holds the title of Corresponding Professor at the University of the Russian Academy of Education in Moscow and works closely with the Faculty of Philosophy at Zhejiang University in China. He is also the coauthor of "Journeys of Discovery," an integrated studies curriculum for schools.

TABLE OF CONTENTS

PREFACE

> *We had the experience but missed the meaning.*
> T.S. Eliot, *The Four Quartets*

This book is designed to help you realize two goals: (a) raising academic achievement, and (b) improving the social/moral fabric of school life. In order to accomplish these two goals we will explore and develop the relationships among three important but seldom connected endeavors: teaching, learning, and assessment. If this effort is successful, you will come to think of the three as inseparable. The idea is that these three elements of school life need to be considered as seamless, they must not be separated. And to the extent that you act on this idea, you will be well on the way toward the development of a reflective classroom. Your classroom will become a place where you and your students think and act reflectively. Your classroom will become a place where thinking, feeling, and doing have meaning. It will be a place where you and your students feel free to express their thoughts in an atmosphere of trust and openness. And for this to happen, first you must imagine it. You must think that this is possible. You must think that this is something worthwhile that you and your students can accomplish.

What would such a classroom be like? How would such a classroom be different from an ordinary classroom? Does it matter *what* you teach? *Who* you teach? I wish to suggest that these questions matter less than *why* you teach. What and who you teach will vary considerably from one teacher to another, but unless you are willing to confront the question of why you teach there is little hope for long-term improvement. The strategies we will develop in this book will work with younger learners as well as older learners. They can be used across a wide range of subject matter areas. And they *will* work. You'll find that several related outcomes will emerge. As you and your students begin to realize the power of these outcomes, you will also realize that a classroom can be a place of energy, fulfillment, and joy.

AN IMPROVED SOCIAL SETTING

Among the outcomes you will experience is an improved social setting. You and your students will know each other better, and you will sense a greater willingness on the part of those present to work together. *Group skills, team building, and cooperation* have been clearly identified as crucial elements of success in the workplace as well as to success in life in general. Study after study informs us that employers are looking for people who genuinely like to work together, who see themselves as connected to others, and who take pleasure in being part of team efforts. The myth of the rugged individual who solves problems apart from the help of others is not only just that, a myth, but it is a dangerous conception as well. All too often we are reminded tragically of the effects of a disconnected, alienated life. Your classroom can be something better. It can be a place where people really get to know one another, where friendships are made, and working together is more typical than not. *Citizenship* is a primary goal of American education, and the quest ought to begin right in your classroom.

A RICHER MORAL FABRIC

Also, you will see a deepened, richer moral fabric in the life of your classroom. When students and teachers begin to think and act *reflectively*, questions of purpose, value, and meaning inevitably arise. There is no turning back. The implications for this are vast. Some students have rarely been asked to consider their own feelings, their own sense of purpose, or their own thoughts of what might be meaningful. As you and your students consider questions of purpose, meaning, and worth, you will come to deeper levels of *self-awareness and awareness of others.* This actually is a very practical thing. A caring "atmosphere is simply a better place in which to work and learn. *Discipline* begins to take on new meaning as you and your students reflect on what it means to be a truly disciplined individual, to be a caring person, to want the best for self and others. And as the moral compass" is engaged, you will experience a kind of *esprit de corps* that transcends the ordinary, that brings people together as a miniature community.

IMPROVED ACADEMIC ACHIEVEMENT

Higher academic achievement will follow. Because you and your students will spend more time writing and speaking about the material you are studying, you will have created a reflective atmosphere, one that enables students to revisit key ideas and skills. You and your students will find yourselves *discovering* new ways to document learning, to keep the record. You will find new ways to raise the *level of consciousness* about the things that are being taught, and learned. Your students will not merely study ideas, they will step outside the process and consider thoughtfully what they are studying. Levels of *reinforcement* will follow that you might not have thought possible. Because you will have developed strategies for integrating assessment with teaching and learning, you will notice a change in your students' test results: the scores will be higher. This is so because your students will experience continuous reinforcement of important ideas as opposed to the business-as-usual approach that separates testing from "normal" classroom activity, saving it, unfortunately, until the end of an experience and presenting it as a disconnected outside event.

And so, if you wish to create a social, moral, and academic setting in which you and your students experience connectedness, search for meaning, and find joy in learning, please read on. It is not a particularly easy journey, not one intended for the easily discouraged. I can assure you that there will be difficulties along the way. This is true of anything worthwhile; and what is more worthwhile than helping young people learn?

TEACHING

Teaching has been defined in a variety of ways, but two useful images give us a place to begin. One image is that of a scholarly or otherwise well-informed individual sharing his/her knowledge and skills with students. The premise is simple: one person knows things that others need to know, and it is the role of that person, the teacher, to somehow get those ideas across to learners. Thus we have an expert working with novices. This is a familiar image. A primary teacher not only knows how to read, but knows how to enable young students to learn to read. And if things go really well, the teacher inspires children to *want* to read. A high school physics teacher must master difficult subject matter, but must also know how to impart the needed concepts and principles of physics to students. And to the extent that the teacher inspires students, this is how we get our next generation of physicists. This is the *traditional* description of the teacher. It is often maligned by progressives as pedantic, dated, and irrelevant to teaching and learning in today's world. But only when didacticism is carried to excess is this the case. In fact, it can be a powerful way to think about the role of the teacher. Its greatest strength, however, also contains its inherent weakness, and that is the temptation to put subject matter ahead of people. When this happens learning becomes impersonal, and the human connections so desperately needed are lost. It is good to remember the old adage, "people first, procedures second, and tools third."

The other way of thinking about teaching is to consider the teacher as *facilitator*. The image is not so much that of the scholar dispensing knowledge as it is of the helpful coach, the fellow learner and guide. This is not to say that the teacher should know nothing, although that is what in fact Socrates claimed about himself. Rather the idea is that of a teacher who wants students to learn for themselves, to explore, discover, construct, and create their own knowledge. Actually, to do this well, a teacher must possess a great deal of knowledge of subject matter, because students need him/her to help them make the necessary connections between and among ideas.

This teacher is less concerned about traditional notions of subject matter and more concerned with project learning, with student sharing and team building, and with applications to the world beyond the school. This is a difficult role for some teachers because they want to "give" their knowledge to young learners. The fact is, though, that this is not possible. Each person must finally construct his/her own knowledge of the world. It is helpful to remember Jean Piaget's statement that "telling is not teaching". Piaget described teaching as the organization of environments in which students' intellectual and social growth can emerge. This means clearly a shift in the center of gravity from teacher to learner.

LEARNING

John Dewey advocated the idea of the teacher becoming a learner and learners becoming teachers. Obviously what he had in mind was a coming together of people and processes where roles become less clearly delineated. Often we have heard insightful teachers speak about how much they learn from their students. In some cases they may be speaking about content or subject matter, and more often probably about the students themselves. In his book, *Small Is Beautiful*, E.F. Schumacher notes that even animals teach us. He points out how much someone learns from a dog, a cow, or other domestic animals. We learn lessons of responsibility, caring, nurture, and most of all patience. At least the potential to learn these things is there. So why would a teacher *not* learn much of value from his/her students?

The Roman orator Seneca noted that "we learn best by teaching." This is so because if we know we must teach something, we now have an additional, more compelling reason for learning it. I will argue in this book that learning should be active, that it is a pursuit. Obviously, if students are making robots from Legos, that is active. If they are putting on a play or a puppet show, that too is active. But even such traditionally "passive" work as reading and listening should be active. Active learning shifts the center of gravity from the "teacher" to the learner. The economist Peter Drucker, writing about schools, notes that nothing much is going to change until schools are willing to cross the frontier from teaching to learning. Drucker's perceptive comment informs us that the best results will happen when the responsibility for learning lies directly with the learner. This has always been true, and it is time to act on it. The key is balance, some of each.

REFLECTIVE ASSESSMENT

I want to mention a term that you no doubt have come across before in your reading, and that term is *metacognition*. Metacognition is a theory that states that learners benefit by thoughtfully and reflectively considering the things they are learning and the ways in which they are learning them. A common phrase used by its advocates is "thinking about thinking." Any attempts at assessment without metacognition are deficient. By testing students in traditional ways, we might find out what they remember about what we think they should remember, but we do not get to truth, meaning, purpose, or utility.

This book focuses on a different sense of what it means to assess. You will find that the metacognitive or reflective thinking strategies found in these pages are small-scale. They are not designed to take the place of standardized tests and other formal ways of finding out what students know. Rather, they are designed to help you and your students toward a practical sense of what works, what is good, what has meaning, and ultimately, *why*. We live in a day of standards, accountability, and formal measures of academic success. They seem to be here to stay. But I wish to suggest that assessment should be something more truthful and fulfilling than these "external" measures are for most students and their teachers. It ought to be enjoyable (yes, I mean that), it ought to improve the social/moral conditions we teach and learn in, and of course it ought to provide some concrete means for raising achievement. Reflective assessment is for everyone, students and teachers alike.

If all goes well, this book will help you to bring teaching, learning, and assessment together into a seamless whole. You will begin to experience a sense of integration with your students, just as they will with you and with each other. You will find that you have created a more truthful, searching, supportive environment. And you should see tangible evidence that the two goals expressed in the book are becoming a reality: raising academic achievement and improving the social/moral fabric of school life.

REFERENCES AND SUGGESTED READINGS

Dewey, J. (1933, 1998). *How we think*. Boston, MA: Houghton Mifflin.

Drucker, P. (1990). *The new realities*. New York: Perennial Library.

Schumacher, E. F. (1989). *Small is beautiful: Economics as if people really mattered*. New York: Harper Collins.

TAKE THIS TEST

The following are a number of statements about teaching and learning. As you respond to them, you'll begin to get an idea of your own preliminary thoughts about some of the ideas contained in this book. When you have finished, just add up your numbers to get a score.

Mark "7" if you Strongly Agree; "3" if you are Not Sure; and "0" if you Strongly Disagree.

_____ School subjects should be taught in an integrated fashion.

_____ The student's role in learning should be active and initiatory.

_____ School learning should be primarily problem-focused.

_____ Students should play an active role in curriculum planning.

_____ Students should be given more time to discuss ideas with each other.

_____ Conversation, construction, and inquiry should receive major emphasis in the school day.

_____ Intrinsic motivation is the key to productive learning.

_____ Students should spend more time reflecting on ideas than mastering skills.

_____ Cooperative work and group projects should predominate.

_____ Students need class time to discuss the meaning and purpose of what they are learning.

_____ Students themselves ought to help decide what they should study.

_____ Student behavior and student interest are closely connected.

_____ The major purpose of assessment ought to be self-assessment.

_____ State and national standards will contribute little to real learning.

_____ Frontal, whole-class teaching should be kept to a minimum.

_____ Less time should be devoted to "covering" the curriculum.

You'll have another opportunity to take the test again after you have become familiar with the practices presented in this book. For now, the higher your score, the more you fit into the "constructivist" camp. The lower your score, the more you fit into what we might call the "traditionalist" camp.

PART I

REFLECTIVE PRACTICE

Let such teach others who themselves excel.
Alexander Pope

1

1

DEVELOPING A
LEARNING CULTURE

> *Reflection is as indispensable to great artists as it is
> to philosophers, diplomats, writers, and scientists.
> Unfortunately, it is infrequently used in schools.*
> Renata and Geoffrey Caine

Teachers and students today have a wide range of teaching/learning strategies from which to choose. These ways to teach and learn include class discussion, teacher presentation, and demonstration, just to name a few teacher-directed strategies; and discovery learning, learning centers, cooperative learning, and project learning, to name a few student-centered approaches. In each case students can be challenged to consider ideas, to venture opinions, to take notes and organize information, and to construct virtual or actual models. When motivating activities are undertaken, high levels of student interest follow, and the possibilities for involvement loom large. The focus of this book is on classroom life and the wider connections that flow from it to home and community. In that sense, it is small-scale. You won't learn in these pages how to restructure a whole system or school. Such policy-level reforms have been the object of great attention in recent times and probably always will be with us. Those who find themselves interested in large-scale topics in education will have no trouble finding sources. I want to visit with you at the level where human beings interact most closely in school life, and that is the level where teachers and students come together in the name of learning.

You will find here a few carefully chosen recurring themes. Those themes are interest, opportunity, and reflection. There is nothing complicated about these themes. Interest is the desire to learn something. Opportunity is a favorable juncture of circumstances. And reflection is the basis of the examined life. I will attempt to show you, using both theory and practice, that when these themes become the reality of classroom life, academic achievement will rise and the social/moral fabric of school life will improve.

3

If your classroom were to become a place where students followed their interests within the course of study, how would it be different from the way things are now? What would happen if you allowed your students to tell you what they planned to do in order to meet the academic requirements you have established? How would you feel if your students began to tell you, consistently, that they really enjoy school?

If your classroom were to become a place of opportunity, what would that mean in a practical sense? If someone were to mention to you that your classroom is a place where choices abound and greater opportunities are found, how would you feel? If you could clearly see that your students know that your classroom is less a place of restriction than one of opportunity, would you welcome this?

If your classroom were to become a place where time is given to reflect, to think, and to analyze, how would it be different? What would happen if you decided to "cover" less ground and spent more time treating a few selected issues in depth? To what extent do you think you would be willing to turn over much of the responsibility for the assessment of academic achievement and the quality of classroom life to your students? What would happen if you did?

Assuming you are willing to take some risks toward a transformed teaching/learning environment, where do you begin? Active learning is a place to begin, but unless it is accompanied by reflective thinking, little meaningful learning will result. This is why activities in themselves, no matter how compelling, are often no more intellectually challenging than traditional "passive" learning. Hands on learning advocates make the point that active student involvement is inherently superior to traditional seatwork, but the evidence in the form of higher test scores is largely lacking. Hands-on learning has little more to commend it than the observation that it is generally more fun than seatwork. I was once told by a Chinese professor, who had spent much time in the United States, that he had observed that when American students wish to compliment an instructor at the end of a course, they typically say how much they enjoyed it. He said that, on the other hand, when Chinese students wish to compliment an instructor, they typically say that they learned a lot. How good it would be to combine the messages!

Permit me to illustrate this thought with an example from my own teaching experience. The first year that I taught, I was always looking for art ideas. From time to time I would go to the library and read books on various art projects in search of activities for my students, ones I thought they would enjoy and profit from. I spent hours looking for lessons that seemed particularly interesting. One that struck my fancy, and the students seemed to agree, was soap carving. You simply take a bar of Ivory Soap and go to work! (Of course there is more to it than that, there are certain skills involved to be sure, and given today's climate one would be considered rather foolish to arm 30 kids with knives anyway, so it doesn't matter.) And so we set about this venture. The students did some rather creative work, I thought, and we displayed their efforts on a table in the back of the room.

This was all to the good. Carving soap is therapeutic and visually expressive at the same time. But the difference between this lesson, which was reasonably good from the standpoint of active involvement and student enjoyment, and one that could have been far better was enormous. What was missing? What would I do differently now? The missing piece, the piece so often missing in the school experience, was reflection, a search for meaning. We never really reflected on the experience. We didn't take the time to talk about sculpture and how carving as artistic expression involves taking away, while painting, in contrast, involves adding to. I didn't think to ask the students to talk about how they felt about their work. We didn't spend time writing or drawing about the experience. We didn't have a potter or sculptor visit the class to talk with young artists about their work. It didn't occur to me to show them examples of sculpture by professional artists or craftsmen. In short, we had the experience but missed the meaning, to paraphrase the poet T.S. Eliot.

This is the essence of reflective thinking, a search for meaning. Reflection involves stepping back from what you're doing in order to achieve some measure of perspective. It means thinking, talking, and otherwise expressing your feelings, the things you've learned, the growth you've achieved, and the sense you have of accomplishing something. I am convinced that this is one of the greatest problems we face in classroom life. The problem is, a failure to reflect. The remedy is to take the time to do it in spite of the fact that you and your students won't be able to "cover" as much. No amount of "fun" activities can make up for the loss that accompanies a failure to search for meaning.

This book is designed to help you with the issues of interest, opportunity, and reflection in teaching and learning. To the extent that you practice the 22 activities found in the second part of this volume, you will begin to see positive changes in your learning environment. You will in all probability see higher achievement by your students. Higher student achievement ought to be the goal in any educational situation. But that alone is not sufficient. I think you will also see an improved social/moral fabric in the daily life of your classroom. As students begin to act on the basis of genuine interest, as they sense the unlimited opportunities available in your classroom, and as they practice reflective self-assessment they in turn become more reflective in their practice, just as you will. Assessment at its best is about far more than test scores, important as they are. Assessment, as I will attempt to prove in these pages, lies at the very heart of learning. My hope is that you will come to think of teaching, learning, and assessment as indivisible.

QUESTIONS FOR DISCUSSION AND REFLECTION ON DEVELOPING A LEARNING CULTURE

♦ Of the three functions (teaching, learning, assessing), which seems least likely to occur routinely?

♦ What do you need to know to be able to combine them more effectively?

REFERENCES AND SUGGESTED READINGS

Brookfield, S. (1995). *Becoming a critically reflective teacher.* San Francisco, CA: Jossey-Bass Publishers.

Caine, R. & G. (1994). *Making connections: Teaching and human brain.* Menlo Park, CA: Addison-Wesley Publishing.

Elliot, T. (1971) *The complete poems and plays, 1909-1950.* New York: Harcourt, Brace & World, Inc.

Palmer, P. (1998). *The courage to teach.* San Francisco, CA: Jossey-Bass Publishers.

2

TWO GOALS OF SCHOOL LIFE

> The foundation of education is to raise children
> to be fine human beings.
> Shinichi Suzuki

It is not uncommon for state and district guides to list numerous goals, objectives, outcomes, and other means of aiming toward improved results. You can select one of these guides virtually at random and find a list of statements that most of us would readily agree with. The problem seldom lies with any given statement; they are invariably laudable. The *problem* is that there are typically so many of them that they defy any rational analysis or reflective thought. The *result* is that they are then ignored, which is unfortunate because we are, or at least ought to be, goal-oriented in a profession such as ours.

People who set a limited number of strategically significant goals are generally far more successful in goal attainment than those who either have no stated goals or who have too many goals to keep reasonable track of. This is true in politics, business, child rearing, school, or any other walk of life. The key is to (a) have a limited number of goals, (b) be certain that the goals you do have are worth believing in, and (c) establish concrete ways of realizing the goals.

I wish to propose only two goals of school life. I am convinced that if you take these two goals seriously, you will see positive, lasting, tangible results. If we limit ourselves to two goals, several things become possible. First of all, it is rather easy to keep track of two goals. Secondly, it is relatively easy to communicate such a limited number of goals to students, parents, and other interested parties. And thirdly, when it comes to measuring goal attainment, wouldn't you rather have two goals to measure rather than the typical dozen or so? What I'm proposing is that we not get lost in the goal structure, which is, more often than not, exactly what happens.

Here are the two goals:

1. Raising academic achievement, and
2. Improving the social/moral fabric of school life.

This is all you need. You do not need a laundry list of aims, objectives, goal statements, etc. In the end, such lists lead inevitably either to frustration or cynicism. Just remember these two important goals and act on them. If you do, and if you have the right kinds of strategies, and if you select powerful ideas for you and your students to consider, then you will be successful. But remember, you have to believe in the importance of the goals. So if I were to ask you how important these two goals are, you would need to tell me that they are *very* important to you as a teacher or administrator.

Let's examine the first goal: *raising academic achievement*. You may be teaching in an environment where test scores are already high. You may be teaching in an environment where the present situation is something less than that. It doesn't matter. Whatever the situation, there is always room for improvement and need for improvement.

The point is that we can always do better no matter who we are. This is true for each individual. High achievers, middle achievers, and low achievers all can and should improve their academic work. This is not meant in a competitive sense. It merely means that you and I and others can always read better literature, learn more mathematics, become more aware of the world in which we live, and so on.

Few of us know everything. This is an exciting idea because it represents opportunity for every learner. We can always learn more because there is no scarcity of ideas in the universe. You cannot exhaust the supply of knowledge because knowledge feeds on itself, creating new knowledge. The more we learn about something worthwhile, the more we are motivated to learn more about it, and this is the secret to raising achievement beyond business as usual. This is how you rise above mediocrity into the transcendent realms of true learning. All learners are capable of breaking the barrier of other-directed learning and becoming self-directed. Madame Maria Montessori called such self-directed learners *autodidacts*, people who learn because they want to learn and have learned how to learn.

The second goal is: *improving the social/moral fabric of school life*. Uncomfortable, crowded conditions are typically the norm in a classroom. Most teachers would prefer to have a larger room, more space for the students to work, and more places to put things. If enrollment in most schools were smaller, if classrooms had fewer students, if school architecture were truly designed for learning, then things would be better than they are. Let us hope these things come to pass. However, it is often the case that there is little we can do about this in any immediate sense. Those who prefer to see the negative side of things no doubt have many problems to point to. But this is why it is productive to turn to other avenues in order to meet this strategic goal.

If we can agree that school life ought to offer students and teachers the opportunity to become self-directed learners, to practice citizenship, to set individuals on the path toward self-realization, to prepare students for a future in the workplace, and to be a place where civility prevails, then we must take this second goal seriously, because it accounts for each of these.

The two strategic goals are inseparable. The more you practice the strategies contained in this book, the more I think you will come to agree with this idea. Academic achievement without morality is not merely hollow; it is dangerous. Morality without academic achievement leaves us with a weak excuse for having school, one that the public will not and should not accept.

CONCLUSION

The key to bringing these two strategic goals of school life into sync is reflective practice. A reflective classroom is by definition a place where the two goals are being taken seriously by all involved. Teaching, learning, and assessment together in the context of reflective practice is our theme. The two goals are practical, attainable goals in almost any given school situation. As you build up the connections between teaching, learning, and assessment, and as you and your students search for significance and meaning in the life of your classroom, two things will happen: (a) you will find that academic achievement will rise, and (b) you will find your classroom to be a more civil, responsible, and moral place in which to work and play.

QUESTIONS FOR DISCUSSION AND
REFLECTION ON TWO GOALS OF SCHOOL LIFE

- ♦ In what ways are the two goals liberating for you? In what ways are they frustrating?

- ♦ To what extent do you believe that reflective strategies will improve achievement as well as the social/moral climate of your classroom?

- ♦ What does the term "social/moral" climate mean to you?

REFERENCES AND SUGGESTED READINGS

Beane, J. (1997). *Curriculum integration*. New York: Teachers College Press.

Bruner, J. (1985). Narrative and paradigmatic modes of thought. In E. Eisner (Ed.), *Learning and teaching the ways of knowing, 84th yearbook, NSSE*. Chicago, IL: University of Chicago Press.

Bruner, J. (1995). *The culture of education.* Cambridge, MA: Harvard University Press.

Kessler, R. (2000). *The soul of education: Helping students find connection, Compassion, and character at school.* Alexandria, VA: Association for Supervision and Curriculum Development.

3

THE REFLECTIVE CLASSROOM

You can have experience without reflection, but
you can't have reflection without experience.
Maria Jacobson

Not long ago I had the occasion to visit a wonderful children's museum, one clearly dedicated to educational purposes. The place holds a wide variety of exhibits in its sizable collection, and the exhibits range from the traditional glass-enclosed showcase type to interactive, hands-on experiential learning opportunities. The museum, as you might imagine, is a popular site for field trips, and it is not at all unusual to see one big yellow bus after another lined up on the streets outside. Teachers and students alike look forward to visiting there, and the museum staff is a talented, knowledgeable group perfectly able and willing to ensure that the visits are educationally worthwhile.

On the particular day that I was there, I found I had some time to watch the students come and go. I was especially curious to know how they approached the task of learning in this place of exceptional sensory opportunity. Two rather different class-sized groups caught my attention in particular.

The first was a class of fifth- or sixth-grade students; I was never sure which because there wasn't time to ask them. They literally entered the museum running, their teacher in pursuit exhorting them to 'slow down a little.' The group quickly got out of my sight, apparently on their way to something of interest. After some time had passed, this same group came back, still at high speed, put their coats on, and left the building. One imagines they saw every exhibit possible. Obviously, they were in a hurry, but they did manage to "cover it all," as one student breathlessly informed me as she grabbed her coat and ran for the exit.

The other group I will tell you about was composed of much younger children. They were, in fact, second-graders. I know this because they told me so. They and their teacher seemed to be in no hurry, and I watched them gather around several exhibit cases of ancient vases and other pottery. Each child had a sketch pad (actually a tablet) and pencil. I watched as they took it upon themselves to make careful drawings of what they viewed.

It occurred to me that this experience allowed them to take in more subtle attributes of line, shape, pattern, perspective, texture, color, size, and so on. I can't say that all the drawings were suitable for framing, but that is not the point. The point is that this was a reflective experience, one in which students spent time *considering* an object worthy of examination. This group of students did not manage to see the entire museum during their visit. In other words, they did not 'cover' the whole place as the older students did. But what do you really learn if you do?

The story I have just told you is a metaphor for the school curriculum and the school experience in general. The twentieth century philosopher Alfred North Whitehead reminds us not to try to teach too many things because learning gets lost when we dedicate ourselves to coverage. The eighteenth century philosopher Jean Rousseau wrote that we should teach less and teach what we do teach well. He also admonished those of us who would teach to slow down the process, to take more time on a few worthwhile things.

So, I ask you to think about the two classes visiting the museum. And as you do, ask yourself about the relative value of their very different learning experiences. All experiences teach us something, but only experiences of quality teach us something worthwhile. What are the implications for the school curriculum? My guess is that you can answer this question on the basis of your own reflection.

CONCLUSION

Invariably, when people are asked to recall something interesting, useful, or lasting, in other words something of high quality, from their own school experience, it will be an in-depth experience, perhaps a project, a concert, a play, or an athletic endeavor. And invariably those experiences, which we deem to be of high quality have another attribute, they tend to be participatory.

We will revisit this theme of reflection and engagement in learning throughout the pages of this book. In the next chapter, we will continue our quest to bring teaching, learning, and assessment together through reflective practice by examining the nature of knowledge.

QUESTIONS FOR DISCUSSION AND REFLECTION ON THE REFLECTIVE CLASSROOM

♦ What is your usual pattern when you visit someplace like a museum?

- ◆ What prevents you from eliminating some of the coverage that may dominate your class at the expense of active engagement of students?

- ◆ To what extent would you guess an observer would conclude that activity and reflection are typical events in your classroom?

REFERENCES AND SUGGESTED READINGS

Bruner, J. (1995). *The culture of education.* Cambridge, MA: Harvard University Press.

Costa, A. & Kallick, B. (2000). *Discovering and exploring habits of mind.* Alexandria, VA: Association for Supervision and Curriculum Development.

Dewey, J. (1937). *Experience and education.* New York: Macmillan.

Ellis, A. (1998). *Teaching and learning elementary social studies* (6th ed.). Boston, MA: Allyn & Bacon.

Ornstein, R. (1972). *The psychology of consciousness.* New York: Viking Press.

Rousseau, J. (1983). *Emile.* New York: Dutton. (Original work published 1762)

Whitehead, A.N. (1961). *The aims of education.* New York: American Library/Mentor Books.

4

THE NATURE OF KNOWLEDGE

It is good to know what, useful to know how,
and splendid to know why.
Angela Rastrelli

The acquisition of knowledge is a central purpose of the school experience. Students come to school to learn, at least that is the hope. Parents send their children there for just that purpose. Teachers dream of higher achievement by their students. Academic knowledge, to be sure, is at the forefront, but knowledge of self and others is also considered an integral part of the process. So it is only proper that we spend some time reflecting on the nature of knowledge and the questions, "What is knowledge?" and "How do we know what we know?" Beyond this lies the question, "What knowledge is of most worth?" Such questions ought to be in the forefront of any teacher's mind each time he/she plans and teaches a lesson, and it is one to be explored by students as well.

Most dictionaries define knowledge as facts, skills, abilities, understandings, etc., of which one has some command. Memory is involved, but so is the ability to make applications. If we were to ask someone, "What is two times four?" we would imagine that person "knows" $2 \times 4 = 8$ from memory, but we would also expect the person to be able to apply it to certain instances, for example, "four stacks of two dollars each." If the person could not make such an application we would reasonably conclude he/she does not have knowledge of this. Such questions deal with the issue of *what* we know. *How* we know is yet another matter.

Basically there are three related ways in which we know what we know. None of them ever functions exclusively of the others simply because human beings are such complex creatures, but for purposes of analysis we will separate them and consider each in turn. They are *knowledge received, knowledge discovered,* and *knowledge constructed* (Thut, 1957).

Philosphically, how we know what we know must be considered apart from such a question as whether our knowledge is accurate. For example, one person might "know" that the world is flat and another "knows" that it is round. Each might possess such knowledge without possessing any means of proving his/her case. And the fact of the matter is, that most of the knowledge we do have is subject to change, probably only approximately accurate, and, one hopes, open to new possibilities.

KNOWLEDGE RECEIVED

We begin with the most common way in which you and I know what we know. We receive knowledge from other sources. A parent or a teacher tells us something. We read something in a book. We see a film or video. These are examples of knowledge received. The basic idea is that someone knows something that you or I do not know, and they teach it to us by showing and telling. This is perhaps the single oldest method of formal instruction. It is based on the premise of *dependence by learners on experts*. If, for example, you know that there are nine planets in our solar system, we can imagine that you were told that by your science teacher, that perhaps you acquired this knowledge by reading a textbook or seeing a film, or that you witnessed a model of the solar system at a museum.

You probably remember learning that $A = \pi r^2$, the formula for computing the area of a circle. Most people learn this formula in middle school. And how did they typically learn it? Most likely, they were *shown* this formula in mathematics class. The teacher introduces the formula, works a problem or two on the board, and asks the class whether there are any questions. This is followed by guided practice and homework from the mathematics textbook. It is a familiar routine. And we all could cite literally hundreds of examples of this type of teaching and learning.

The very attractive aspect of knowledge received also contains its potential danger, and that is its appearance of efficiency. You can dispense a great deal of information in one lecture. A social studies textbook chapter can include the geography of several nations or several decades of history. A few pages in a science textbook can explain the entire process of photosynthesis or tell you how the universe was formed. No wonder we look to this way of knowing what we know as the basis of the school curriculum! But keep in mind the old saying, "If something seems too good to be true, it probably is."

The inherent problems of knowledge received, valuable as it is when considered judiciously, are twofold: (a) such knowledge is not one's own, that is, it is imposed and comes from a source outside the learner, and therefore must basically be taken on trust; and (b) such knowledge tends to be abstract and based largely on words and symbols as opposed to the reality of the phenomenon itself. These are the seeds of enormous pedagogical problems. As efficient as this mode of knowing seems, it actually gets in the way of learning in many instances. And the problem is compounded with schoolchildren because they lack the experiential frame of reference needed to make sense of abstract knowledge.

So, while it is true that most of what you and I know is knowledge received, this is not necessarily a good thing. This is especially the case when knowledge received becomes the *heart* of the curriculum experience. Balance is the key, and to achieve balance, we must look to the other two ways of knowing as crucial teaching/learning partners of knowledge received.

 Look ahead: Clear and Unclear Windows (p. 72), Jigsaw (p. 78), Learning Illustrated (p. 92), Key Idea Identification (p. 102)

KNOWLEDGE DISCOVERED

The psychologist Jean Piaget once noted that telling is not teaching. His point was that teaching is a far more complex act than the mere telling and dispensing of information would imply. Piaget preferred to think of teaching as the organization of environments in which students' cognitive and affective structures could emerge and grow. For that to happen, knowledge must be something that one acquires oneself. Experience, not mere verbiage, is the key. Words and symbols are needed, of course, but they are insufficient. They should follow experience and emerge from it. John Dewey noted on more than one occasion that one of the greatest mistakes made by teachers is that of assuming experience on the part of learners when the experience simply does not exist.

More recently, the constructivist paradigm informs us that no one can "give" another person his/her knowledge. Each of us constructs our own knowledge. In socially oriented environments where people live and work together, much of the knowledge becomes shared knowledge. We see this in stories told and retold within the circle of a family, for example, the time Uncle Elmo broke his arm falling out of a swing at the family reunion picnic, or some similar tale. A culture by definition has shared knowledge. But each individual within a family, culture, or society still has his/her own unique sense of that knowledge. The individual's knowledge becomes part of the mosaic of shared, communal knowledge.

This is one reason why students must be allowed to talk and work together in school settings. As individuals share their perceptions with others, the "truth" of situations begins to emerge. If students are given opportunities to reflect on the meaning, the difficulty, or the enjoyment of what they are doing, then a more accurate (truthful) sense of how "things are going" is achieved. It is a very practical thing to do.

We adapt new information to fit our experience, and each of us has different experiences. This is why no two people will get the same thing out of the same activity, lecture, film or story. We are discoverers by nature, and learn best by and from experience. We assimilate new knowledge into the context of what we already know, and we adapt that knowledge in ways that seem reasonable to us.

So, when Piaget described teaching as the organizing of environments, this suggests to us that good teachers will establish settings where *discovery through experience* is at the core. This translates to learning centers, project learning, hands-on experience, teamwork, and other means appropriate to a given age group. The emphasis shifts from *teaching*, in the traditional sense of presentation by the teacher, to *learning* by students. This is a tremendous change, a complete shift in the center of gravity and it should not be underestimated as a transformation of the environment. It is the pedagogical equivalent of crossing a frontier.

The curriculum may be basically the same on the surface. Students may, for example, be learning about the seasons, the Pythagorean theorem, or about our political system. But instead of being *told* how these things work, they are encouraged to use discovery methods, in other words, to *find out for themselves*. To learn about the seasons might require gathering leaves, flowers, and seeds, as well as taking temperatures each day, measuring precipitation, plotting sun angles, recording the times of sunrises and sunsets, and keeping diaries and journals of the information. To learn about our political system, students can participate in student government and become involved in some way in the community in order to discover how the processes work.. In both instances, there would be a certain amount of explaining, informing, and so on, by the teacher, and reading as well as accessing other information sources, but the point is that such information is attached to the discovery process and it is pursued for a reason. When knowledge is discovered, ownership follows because the *responsibility* for learning rests with the learner.

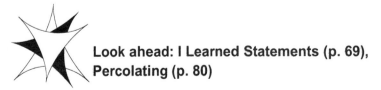

Look ahead: I Learned Statements (p. 69),
Percolating (p. 80)

KNOWLEDGE CONSTRUCTED

Knowledge discovered is about finding out. A student *discovers* that chalk is softer than slate, that democracy is more complex than autocracy, that teamwork requires social skills, that creative writing is different from technical writing, that sculpture is a process of "taking away" while painting involves "adding on," and so on. People of authority could have saved us all a lot time by telling these things to young learners. But the problem, we know, is that the knowledge goes in one ear and out the other. The ancient Chinese proverb says, "I hear and I forget, I see and I remember; I do and I understand." Discovery is not a new idea, but it is a great idea.

There is yet another way in which we know what we know. This way of knowing is that of *knowledge as a human construction*. If knowledge received is represented by "being told," and knowledge discovered is represented by "finding out," then knowledge constructed is represented by "building and creating." The first two types of knowledge represent knowledge that is pre-existent, that is, it is already in place, and the job of the learner is either (a) to be informed by authority or (b) to find out for him/herself. Knowledge as a human construction is different. It tends to be original. It is *constructed* by the learner. It now exists whereas previously it did not. This is not to say that all knowledge constructed is completely original in every respect. However, if a student writes a poem, or builds a project, or paints a picture, then we can think of the effort as knowledge constructed. If a group writes and puts on a puppet show, if a group performs an original dance number, or if a class searches for the truth of conditions in their classroom, then we can think of such efforts as knowledge constructed.

The more students are encouraged to create, to build, to construct, to express themselves, the better they become at it, especially with expert coaching. Knowledge constructed is of course something that can be taken quite literally, a student builds a model house or makes a clay pot of original design. But knowledge constructed is also present when students are invited to critique their own work, to reflect on the meaning of school experience, and to distill the essence of what they are learning. A classroom represents a complex social system with many unique elements at its core. For teachers and students to discuss, reflect, plan, review, and seek the truth of their experience represents some of the finest construction work possible.

The construction of knowledge by students is empowering. It places great authority and control in the hands of the learner(s). It also represents the taking on of responsibility. If for, example, a student decides to construct a model of an Aztec pyramid or of the *Mayflower*, then there is responsibility for attention to authenticity, detail, and design. If a group decides to write and produce an episode from the Lewis and Clark travels, then similar responsibilities must be accepted by the group.

Finally, there is the construction of the knowledge of assessment. It is not enough to make models, write poems, paint pictures, and so on, even though these are fine examples of knowledge constructed. These are experiences that demand reflection, a search for meaning, and satisfaction. This business of reflective assessment may strike you as a less tangible example of knowledge constructed by learners, but it is empowering, emancipating, and needed.

CONCLUSION

Each way of knowing explained here is eminently worth pursuing in school settings. But balance must be kept in mind. What happens when the school experience and knowledge acquisition are based almost exclusively on being told either by teacher or text? This is all too often the case. The search for balance means honoring all three ways of knowing to the extent that all three are prominent. Students who discover, build, and create, but who seldom are required to read, are impoverished. This is why the secret to good writing is that you have to read a lot of good writing. When a student expresses him/herself in writing, this is an act of construction, but the balance is found when the coaching is there, when the reading is required, and when discovery about self and others is encouraged along the way. And whatever form knowledge takes in a school setting, the need for reflection and the continuous re-construction of the experience is necessary.

When balance is achieved, when reflective thinking is taken seriously, when teachers act on the premise that the frontier from teaching to learning must be crossed, great things begin to happen. We witness the transformation of the classroom from a place of top-down authority and emphasis on information and skills, to a place of empowerment and the search for ideas and values.

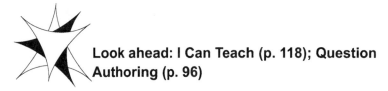

Look ahead: I Can Teach (p. 118); Question Authoring (p. 96)

QUESTIONS FOR DISCUSSION AND REFLECTION ON THE NATURE OF KNOWLEDGE

♦ What is the nature of most of the knowledge emphasized in schools?

♦ What do you think would be an appropriate balance?

♦ What is the role of reflective thinking in each of the three ways of knowing?

REFERENCES AND SUGGESTED READINGS

Armstrong, T. (2000). *Multiple intelligences in the classroom.* Alexandria, VA: Association for Supervision and Curriculum Development.

Brandt, R. (Ed.). (2000). *Education in a new era, ASCD Yearbook 2000.* Alexandria, VA: Association for Supervision and Curriculum Development.

Dewey, John (1933, 1960). *How we think.* Boston, MA: Houghton Mifflin Company.

Freiberg, J. (Ed.). (1999). *Perceiving, behaving, and becoming: Lessons learned.* Alexandria: Association for Supervision and Curriculum Development.

Maslow, A. (1987). *Motivation and personality* (3rd ed.). New York: Harper & Row.

Plato (1991). *The republic.* Chicago: Encyclopaedia Britannica.

Quintilian. (1965). In J. Murphy (Ed.). (J.S. Watson, Trans.). *On the early education of the citizen-orator: Institutio Oratoria.* Indianapolis, IN: Bobbs-Merrill.

Thut, I. (1957). *The story of education.* New York: McGraw Hill.

5

WAYS TO LEARN

> Learn all you can.
>
> Thomas Jefferson's advice
> to Lewis and Clark

JEROME BRUNER'S LEARNING MODES

The psychologist Jerome Bruner describes three learning modes that, taken together, bring balance to the curriculum and variety to the experiences through which teachers and students explore ideas, solve problems, and reflect on meaning. Bruner calls these three learning modes enactive, iconic, and symbolic. *Enactive learning* is basically learning by doing. Another name for this type of learning is experiential learning. *Symbolic learning* is well known and widely practiced, perhaps too much so. Reading, writing, and mathematics, when it is text-driven, are examples of symbolic learning. *Iconic learning* is found somewhere between enactive and symbolic forms. As the term icon implies, pictorial or graphic representation is the key. Thus, pictures, graphs, maps, film, video, CD-ROM's, drawings, and so on, are the ways in which iconic representation is expressed. Thus, iconic learning is not as abstract as symbolic learning, but it is not as experiential as enactive learning.

Bruner's argument is that all three are necessary. The school experience should be one in which appropriate balance is found. All too often, the school day is dominated by symbolic learning, while the other two modes play a greatly diminished role. Symbolic learning, in the form of reading, writing, listening to teacher talk, and so on, is useful, but symbolic representation depends for much of its power on the nature of the experience a learner brings to it. And as many an enlightened educator has warned us, it is not at all helpful to assume experience on the part of children and adolescents because it is so often lacking in their young lives. An unpredicted but very real outcome of the standards movement is a retreat by teachers to a narrow perimeter of "basic skills" teaching using symbolic learning forms, thus unwittingly denying students the very hands-on, active experiences they so desperately need.

So, for example, if a student is expected to read about Japan in a social studies textbook, the chances are good that he/she will gain very little true understanding unless the reading is enriched through such experiences as seeing a film about Japan, constructing Japanese art forms such as origami, and other iconic and enactive encounters. Or imagine the intellectual and social poverty of students who are limited to reading about saving the environment compared to those students whose teacher organizes an environmental study in which students take water and air samples, do fish and bird counts, make their own maps of the area under study, and otherwise become actively engaged in the investigation. On the other hand, imagine the intellectual poverty of actually trying to restore the environment without reading about the issues. So the argument is for balance, true balance.

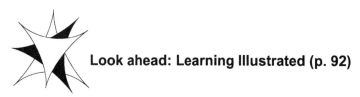

Look ahead: Learning Illustrated (p. 92)

The key to balance is ensuring that all students learn through all three modes. Each mode supports the others in ways that bring about an ecology of learning that is truly symbiotic. Thus, when a unit is in the planning stages, and teachers and students are figuring the ways in which they will approach issues, it is useful to think of ways to balance activities so that equal representation occurs.

MULTIPLE INTELLIGENCES THEORY

Howard Gardner's work in the field of multiple intelligences theory is also an instructive way to think about how people learn. Gardner feels, as many others have, that the traditional view of intelligence is too restrictive, too limiting. His research in a variety of contexts led him to challenge the prevailing wisdom of intelligence as mainly paper and pencil, abstract abilities, and so on. Out of his investigations came the idea that intelligence manifests itself in at least eight distinctly different ways, perhaps more. The eight forms of intelligence that Gardner has identified to date (presently, he is investigating yet another type of intelligence, one that he calls "practical") are described in the following figure.

HOWARD GARDNER'S PRACTICAL INTELLIGENCES

Gardner states that "multiple intelligences is more than a theory of intelligence; it is, for us, a philosophy about education with implications for how kids learn, how teachers should teach, and how schools operate...." (Hoerr, p. 30) His comment serves as a reminder that we need to be far more open than we have been to the possibilities. The message for the classroom is to encourage and support multiple forms of learning and knowing. For starters, this means a lot more artwork, music, construction, projects, teamwork, and, of course, reflective thinking activities.

Look ahead: The Week in Review (p. 76); Search for Meaning (p. 106)

Gardner's eight different intelligences represent a kind of talent pool waiting to be tapped by teachers. Why would we want all our students to be, for example, linguistically intelligent only? It would make for a dull classroom and a dull world. Of course, all the intelligences are held to a certain extent by all students. We are talking here about points of emphasis. And of course, all students need to be challenged to use and develop all the intelligences. The point is that we err when we limit our own view of intelligence to narrow traditional forms, denying the other abilities that human beings have. To the extent that a teacher recognizes, rewards, and emphasizes all eight kinds of intelligence (and Gardner hypothesizes that there may well be more), classrooms become places of opportunity rather than places of restriction.

Look ahead: Circle Meeting (p. 122)

HOWARD GARDNER'S MULTIPLE INTELLIGENCES

1. **Linguistic intelligence** which involves sensitivity to the meaning of words, their order and syntax, the sounds, rhythms, and inflections of language, and the uses of languages.

2. **Musical intelligence** which consists of sensitivities to rhythm, pitch, and timbre. It also has an emotional component. Gardner relates musicians' descriptions of their abilities that emphasize an individual's natural feel for music and not the reasoning or linguistic components of musical ability.

3. **Logical-mathematical intelligence** that emerges from interaction with objects. By a sequence of stages the person is more able to perform actions on objects, understand the relations among actions, make statements about actions, and eventually see the relations among those statements.

4. **Spatial intelligence**, which is the capacity to perceive the physical world, accurately, to perform transformations and modifications on these perceptions, and to produce or recreate forms.

5. **Bodily-kinesthetic intelligence** which involves a person's ability to use the body in highly specific ways, both for expression (the dancer) and goal-directed (the athlete) purposes.

Personal intelligence which takes two forms:

6. *Intrapersonal intelligence* is the ability to access one's own feelings and to label, discriminate, and symbolically represent one's range of emotions in order to understand behavior.

7. *Interpersonal intelligence* involves the ability to notice and make distinctions about others' moods, temperaments, motivations, and intentions.

8. **Naturalist intelligence** is the ability to draw on features of the natural world to solve problems (the chief, gardener, florist).

Gardner theorizes that each form of intelligence has its own unique neurological pattern and its own course of development. If this is so, then it is obvious that different students would exhibit different patterns of doing, feeling, thinking, and reflecting. Such differences should be viewed by teachers as a positive thing because this means a classroom filled with different ways of responding to ideas, of taking action, and of problem solving. Of course, it means as well a multitude of talents, interests, and abilities. So for the teacher who wishes to emphasize collaborative, project-based learning, the potential is enriched greatly because of these differences.

CONCLUSION

Bruner and Gardner are both arguing for some kind of reasonable balance in the learning equation. We have known for some time that traditional paper and pencil approaches to learning, while valuable, are simply too restrictive. Students will enter a complex world where a working knowledge of a wide variety of approaches to learning will be greatly to their advantage. Many of the skills needed in life are either ignored or given little emphasis in schools. Examples of this are Gardner's two forms of personal intelligence. They represent qualities crucial to success in life.

Bruner reminds us that words and symbols represent only one of three major roads of access for the learner. The other two, hands-on activity and iconic representation of ideas, need to be given parity as you and your students plan and carry out learning experiences.

QUESTIONS FOR DISCUSSION AND REFLECTION ON WAYS TO LEARN

♦ Which modes of learning do you typically choose for your own learning?

♦ Choose a student in your class who often struggles, and think of that person in terms of balancing modes of learning. What does that reveal about what that student needs?

♦ What are the implications of multiple intelligences theory for classroom practice? What would be some of the more dramatic changes that would take place if teachers were to emphasize multiple intelligences theory in their classrooms?

♦ Look ahead to the reflective strategies found in the second half of this book. To what extent do they emphasize different learning modes and different intelligences?

REFERENCES AND SUGGESTED READINGS

Armstrong, T. (2000). *Multiple intelligences in the classroom*. Alexandria, VA: Association for Supervision and Curriculum Development.

Beane, J. (1990). *A middle school curriculum: From rhetoric to reality*. Columbus, OH: National Middle School Association.

Bruner, J. (1990). *Acts of meaning*. Cambridge, MA: Harvard University Press.

Gardner, H. (1999). *Intelligence reframed: Multiple intelligences for the 21st century*. New York: Basic Books.

Noddings, N. (1992). *The challenge to care in schools*. New York: Teachers College Press.

Salovey, P. & Sluyter, D. (1997). *Emotional development and emotional intelligence*. New York: Basic Books.

6

SOME USEFUL TEACHING/LEARNING CONCEPTS

> *We ought to employ all the aids of understanding, imagination, sense, and memory…in order to discover the truths.*
>
> Rene Descartes

In this chapter, we examine six concepts designed to serve as reminders of what ought to be happening in a classroom environment that is both active and reflective. These concepts need to be kept in the forefront of your mind and discussed with your students as well. If you are a part of a teaching team, I recommend that you and your partners use them as touch points for planning and reflection.

The six concepts under consideration are:

1. Complexity and chaos;
2. Discipline and creativity;
3. Connection and reflection;
4. Collaboration and team building;
5. Morality and meaning; and
6. Affiliation and projects.

Each of the concepts is closely related to the others, and a great amount of overlap should and does occur among them. They are not a list from which to pick and choose if your goals are to raise achievement and to create an improved social/moral fabric. All of them must be employed with consistency for this to happen because they are supportive one of another. Let's examine each of them in turn.

COMPLEXITY AND CHAOS

At first glance, this concept may seem less than desirable to you. Who wants a complex, chaotic environment when simplicity and order are obviously easier on one's nerves? My answer is that you will, if you'll allow me to explain the idea. Complexity is inevitably a part of higher level thinking, problem solving, and creative expression. The world is itself a complex system made up of innumerable interrelated components. So is a classroom where excellence is present. Attempts to simplify the system by having students keep to themselves, do their own work, refrain from talking, sit in rows, and do worksheets or their equivalent are recipes for drudgery, boredom, and a desire to escape. When complexity is introduced into the system the following changes begin to occur: students are moving about the room, talking to one another, working together on problems, and taking on larger issues involving the use of knowledge and skills as tools rather than merely as ends in themselves.

Now let's add a little chaos to the system. Chaos theory implies that in any system, seemingly random events will occur that effect the entire system in some way. I am sure you are familiar with the idea that if a bluebird flaps its wings in an Idaho forest, the effects ripple outward toward the Caribbean Sea and are felt there, however slightly. The chaos that results from the introduction of complexity into your environment implies two things. First, if you are willing to allow a certain amount of chaos in your classroom, then you are also willing to admit that you do not have a desire to control every event, every interaction that takes place there, in short to micromanage. This is a frightening thought for some teachers. Secondly, this implies that encounters will occur among and between students that are spontaneous, unrehearsed, and *real*. When such things happen, there is great hope for improvement.

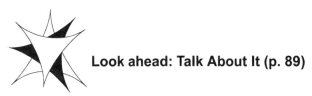 **Look ahead: Talk About It (p. 89)**

DISCIPLINE AND CREATIVITY

The dictionary lists several definitions of the word discipline. The one I wish to emphasize here is "self-control and awareness of others." The sociologist Emile Durkheim, in his book *Moral Education,* offered some of the most profound insights ever into a well-disciplined classroom environment. Durkheim based his ideas of discipline on belief. If teachers and students believe that the work they are doing is important, almost sacred in a sense, then the idea of discipline is lifted up to a higher realm. If each individual believes that he or she is privileged to study great ideas and to work with others in the pursuit of those ideas, then self-discipline must logically follow.

How does a class achieve this? First of all, it certainly won't happen unless you talk about it and get people to express their feelings. And don't underestimate the positive effects of your own rhetorical skills to persuade your students to want what is desirable. Secondly, it will happen when teachers themselves model a sense of excitement, enthusiasm, and, yes, self-discipline. One sees this phenomenon often in the extra curriculum. It is rather common there, in fact. Good coaches of athletics, drama, and debate; good band and choir directors; good art, music, and journalism teachers, all exhibit such traits as genuine knowledge of what they teach, a combination of self-control and enthusiasm, confidence in those whom they lead, and *esprit de corps*. The curriculum needs to learn from the extra curriculum.

Why link creativity with discipline? Simply because truly creative people are more often than not disciplined people. Of course, discipline is not enough. But it offers hope for creativity to emerge. Complex systems theory, as I have noted elsewhere, suggests that for a system to prosper there must be a clear and understandable sense of order, based on a few simple rules, acting as an anchor to the system. The theory also suggests that this sense of order must be balanced with a clear sense of openness at the top of the system in order for individuals and groups to express themselves freely and creatively. Anything less than this causes the system to degrade. Thus discipline in the form of self-control and awareness of others serves as the base, while openness at the top encourages creativity. A final note concerning creativity, surveillance kills it. You have to allow a certain level of freedom, freedom of movement, freedom of thought, and freedom of expression. It's worth the risk.

CONNECTION AND REFLECTION

Good teaching and learning are rarely achieved on the basis of a series of disconnected lessons, even if each individual lesson has some positive qualities. The best teachers refuse to teach out of context. They search for and build connections from one day to the next, from one idea to another, across the disciplines, and out to the world at large. Curriculum developer Jim Beane refers to this higher level of teaching and learning as "integrated studies," in the sense that experiences take on a kind of seamless quality. As teachers do this, their students, sensing that this is how learning best proceeds, will follow.

The elementary school schedule is actually based on this premise, although it is safe to say that the premise is violated when teachers make little or no attempt to connect reading with science, mathematics with social studies, and so on, at the very least. At middle school levels, great progress has been made in recent years toward building connections through block scheduling, team teaching, and integrated studies. And even those secondary teachers who teach a single subject know that for that subject to come alive, it must be related to other subjects, used as an instrument for solving problems, and connected to real world issues.

Reflection is the vehicle for knowing to what extent connections are being made. Reflective practice in the form of journal entries, class and small group discussions, and the other strategies found in this book are designed to draw this out. Reflective practice raises the fundamental questions:

♦ "To what extent does the work we are doing as a class connect to the work I am doing as an individual?"

♦ "How does the work we have done up to this point connect to our present efforts and into the future?" "Are we connecting our school work to the world around us?"

♦ "Can I offer examples of how I could use the skills and knowledge we are learning?"

♦ "To what extent are we really working together?" "How truthful, beautiful, or practical are the things we are learning?"

♦ "In what ways does our schoolwork touch the lives of others?"

Reflection, a quality so often missing in our hurry to 'get things done," is like a ship's compass. We need to turn to it regularly in order to ensure that we are steering the true course.

Look ahead: Write It Down (p. 112)

COLLABORATION AND TEAM BUILDING

To the extent that you can develop an attitude of "we're in this together," you will have succeeded in realizing this concept. Again, I will point to the extra curriculum for the best examples. Musicians in a band or orchestra know that every player, every instrument, is necessary to ensure the success of a performance. And the key beyond that simple fact is the integration of the effort. The same thing is true in a play production. Every role, from leading actor or actress to bit player to stage hand, is crucial.

Synergy is created when people integrate their efforts toward a common goal. A dynamic effect occurs that, as Gestalt theory suggests, is greater than the sum of its parts. It is tempting to point toward the lone problem solver as a model, but the truth is that this is more myth than fact. We can say, for example, that Thomas Jefferson wrote the *Declaration of Independence*. Yes, he did, but with a great deal of help from Benjamin Franklin, James Madison, and even John Locke, on whose *Declaration of the Rights of Man*, Jefferson based his work. And Jefferson himself would have been the first to tell you that he was expressing the ideas and feelings of a large number of revolutionary thinkers of his time and place. Even most successful writers and artists who "work alone" are, in fact, part of a community of people and ideas.

On a more practical note, the writer James Goleman, author of the book, *Emotional Intelligence in the Workplace,* makes a clear and convincing case that those who will succeed in the workplace of the future are those who understand and are willing to act on team building, group effort, and collaboration. There is plenty of room for independent study in school life. But there is really no reason for independent study to be separated from the integrated life of the classroom. You may read one book and I may read another as a way of fulfilling our responsibilities, but we are both enriched if we have the chance to discuss our readings together.

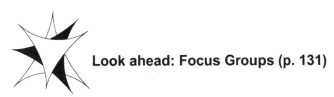 **Look ahead: Focus Groups (p. 131)**

MORALITY AND MEANING

The great leader of the Indian independence movement, Mohandas Gandhi, noted that among mankind's worst sins are knowledge without character, friendship without trust, and promises without fulfillment. But just try a little experiment. Remove the "out" from each "without" and what do you have? You have a goal structure for the moral life of school!

A classroom at its best is a place of honesty, where people feel free, even invited, to speak their mind in an atmosphere of mutual respect and support. Anything less than that represents an atmosphere of restraint and lack of respect for the feelings and thoughts of those directly involved. In the introduction, I mentioned John Dewey's belief that among students' natural tendencies is a desire to converse with one another and to express themselves in a variety of ways. Unless these two conditions are met, you cannot have a morally uplifting environment. In the *Bible*, there is a passage that states, "speak the truth and the truth shall set you free." The operative words are "speak," "truth," and "free." The three words are linked wisely together, and the message for the classroom is clear. If you wish to have an environment of morality then you need to begin the process by opening up conditions to the point that time and consideration are given for students to think aloud, to express their ideas, to relate their feelings, and to build each other up.

It is not uncommon for teachers to express a desire to teach students things that are meaningful to them. But a common error is for teachers to assume that certain things are meaningful to students when they may or may not be. And in the last analysis, only the person or persons for whom meaning is intended can decide whether meaning is present. We can say that it is meaningful for students to study algebra, but how do we know this is so? The only way I know of to determine meaning in the lives of others is to search for it: to ask, to observe, to listen, to care. All of this takes time, and it becomes a moral choice whether we want to give students time (that might otherwise have been used to "cover" more subject matter) to discuss, reflect, and search for meaning in the curriculum.

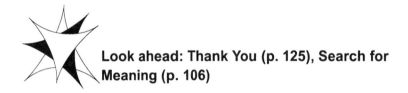

Look ahead: Thank You (p. 125), Search for Meaning (p. 106)

AFFILIATION AND PROJECTS

Perhaps you're wondering how these two concepts ever got paired in my mind. I think they naturally go together. Let me tell you why. Affiliation is a sense of belonging—of being involved. It implies membership in the group, being part of things. Projects, so psychologists tell us, are something we are literally wired to do. As human beings, we naturally think in terms of projects, things we need to get done, to accomplish, and to do well. Projects are, by their very nature, complex enterprises. They call on knowledge, skills, and values as instruments to be used in solving problems and getting things done. Great projects demand much from us and we need help in order to do them well. In my mind, this is where the connection between affiliation and projects begins.

Projects are integrative, that is, they call on knowledge as a tool, not as an end in itself, and they are, at best, team efforts. In his excellent book, *Curriculum*

Integration, James Beane writes, "Thinking...about the integration of knowledge and its use as an instrument for addressing real problems is one sign of a deeper meaning behind the idea of curriculum integration, namely, its possibilities for helping to bring democracy to life in schools." (1997, p. 8) Beane identifies two salient characteristics of the project approach and of American education in general: integration and democracy. The driving force behind a meaningful project is that we actually want to see it through, not just learn information for a test or some other artificial outcome. This makes all the difference in the world. If students are working together to put on a puppet show, then the project takes on a life of its own, from designing the theatre and costumes to the production itself. Knowledge, skills, and values are actually put to use to solve a practical problem. Teamwork is needed, and so are different skills, interests, and abilities. Finally, we realize that we have done more than integrate knowledge into useful forms; we have integrated people, which is the basis of democracy. Good projects serve as "opportunity creators." They create the opportunities to become involved, affiliated, a part of things; opportunities to do something meaningful.

Look ahead: Parents on Board (p. 128), Get a Job (p. 137), Authentic Applications (p. 134)

CONCLUSION

These six concepts are offered for your consideration as ways to reflect on the course you and your students will follow. You have to ask yourselves whether you have chosen a true course, where you want to go, how you want to get there, and what it might mean if you do. It may be helpful for you to think of the concepts themselves as guideposts, trail markers, even a map of the rugged terrain. If these concepts become real, internalized, a part of classroom life, then they will have served an educational purpose.

Try not to think of the concepts as material or ideas only for teachers. I think you should share them with your students. You need to talk about them, mentioning the strategies by name. The terms need to become part of your vocabulary and your students' vocabularies as well. Socrates advocated a life filled with reflection. He went so far as to say that anything less is a life unfulfilled. I will paraphrase him by saying that a school experience without clear, conceptual points of reference is something less than it might otherwise have been.

QUESTIONS FOR DISCUSSION AND REFLECTION

♦ What risks are involved in giving up the "coverage" mentality in order to pursue these reflective concepts? Are the risks worth the effort?

♦ How comfortable are you sharing your reflections with your students? How comfortable are they sharing with each other?

REFERENCES AND SUGGESTED READINGS

Ausubel, D. (1963). *The psychology of meaningful verbal learning.* New York: Grune & Stratton.

Bandura, A. (1971). *Social learning theory.* New York: General Learning.

Chomsky, N. (1966). *Cartesian linguistics: A chapter in the history of rationalist thought.* New York and London: Harper & Row.

Dewey, J. (1910, 1998). *How we think.* Boston, MA: Houghton Mifflin.

Jensen, E. (1998). *Teaching with the brain in mind.* Alexandria, VA: Association for Supervision and Curriculum Development.

Joyce, B. & Weil, M. (2000). *Models of teaching* (6th ed.). Boston, MA: Allyn and Bacon.

Piaget, J. & Inhelder, B. (1968). *The psychology of the child.* New York: Basic Books.

Schiefele, U., Krapp, A., & Winteler, A. (1992). Interest as a Predictor of Academic Achievement: A Meta-analysis of Research. In K. A. Renninger, S. Hidi, & A. Krapp (Eds.), *The role of interest in learning and development.* Hillsdale, NJ: Erlbaum.

Vygotsky, L. (1978). *Mind in society.* Cambridge, MA: Harvard University Press.

7

WHY ASSESS TEACHING AND LEARNING

> I watched the child without interrupting her, and counted
> how many times she would do her work over and over.
>
> Maria Montessori

There are those, a small minority admittedly, who oppose any formal attempts to assess school learning. Their position is basically that such efforts erode trust and other relational qualities between teachers and students. They note that students are told to learn for the joy of learning, and just about the time they take us seriously, we destroy the experience by testing them. Further, they cite the damage done to the self-image of those who do poorly on tests. Is it worth it, they ask, to hurt people in the name of finding out what they know? There is definitely something to these criticisms. As critics of formal testing so often point out, school is the only place in the world where you have to be tested so often, so publicly, and so artificially.

Many students and teachers have an "objectified" sense of assessment, one based on experience. That is, they view tests as separate events or objects set apart from learning and teaching. This is, in fact, the traditional model of assessment. We've all heard the dire warning, "don't forget, the test will be on Friday," or something to that effect. Young children, who tend to view the world as a whole rather than a collection of parts, are especially confused with traditional testing procedures. After all, they have been busy learning to do real things like riding bicycles and learning the rules of games, important things, without being subjected to paper and pencil tests over what they've learned.

The question I've posed about assessment is, why do it? I really think it is a fair question for students and teachers to ask of themselves and each other. To do it because we've always done it is not a sufficient reason. I want to give you some reasons why we should assess teaching and learning, but before we get into them, I do need to make one thing clear, and that is that the more you can bring teaching, learning, and assessment together, the more successful you and your students will become in knowing how and to what extent meaningful progress is being made.

Some reasons for assessing teaching and learning are (a) to classify students, (b) to diagnose students, and (c) to encourage and support student learning.

TO CLASSIFY STUDENTS

One reason for assessing student achievement is to *classify* or *grade* students. Whether it is a compelling reason is debatable; nevertheless, one job of the schools is to determine who has learned sufficiently to be awarded promotions, diplomas, entrance to university, and so on. Without such information we simply could not sort students on the basis of their achievements. Terms like excellence, mediocrity, and failure would have no school-related meaning.

TO DIAGNOSE STUDENTS

A second reason is *diagnostic*. Without some means of assessment, we would have no way of making meaningful referrals to remedial, gifted, or other programs. Diagnostic tests, expert opinion, and other means of diagnosis are often used to place students in situations where their academic needs are best met. I have mentioned elsewhere in these pages that I only wish we were as interested in assessing student strengths as we seem to be in assessing their weaknesses!

TO ENCOURAGE AND SUPPORT STUDENT LEARNING

A third reason for assessment is to *encourage and support student progress*. Most of us want to know from time to time how we are doing. We would like to know that we can do certain things better, that we know more about something, that our insights have deepened. One way in which we can have some assurance of these matters is to document our growth through some means of record keeping (see this strategy) and assessment. Assessment going in gives us some idea, however rough, of where we are, and assessment along the way and at the end of an experience gives us some idea of how far we've come. In other words, the purpose of assessment in this context is self-knowledge and feedback.

I don't mean to minimize these first three reasons, and there is plenty of help out there for you if you wish to pursue these ideas. The last time I checked, and that was quite recently, there was no shortage of measurement and assessment textbooks available. Instead, I wish to dwell on a rationale for assessment that integrates it with teaching and learning. In that sense, my concern is with small-scale assessment as a seamless part of classroom life. So, please consider assessment as inseparable from teaching and learning in a world where all three come together naturally.

The best assessment is that which leads to the improvement of individuals and groups. Without this perspective, there is little hope of excellence. If a child is a mediocre speller and has the potential and the desire to become a good speller, then we ought to do what we have to do to make it happen. If a student is a great natural musician, one who loves music, then the question becomes, "what can we do to provide challenging opportunities for that student?" If a group of students is struggling with a performance and we can document some reasons why that is so, then we ought to act decisively to improve things. In each case, the best assessment will be a combination of expert judgment and input from the person(s) affected.

I think that you will find that the 22 strategies found in these pages are helpful in this regard. If you and your students act on them, *achievement will improve*, and this is true regardless of where people are on the achievement scale, from low to high.

Beneath the desire and the means to improve, however, there is another issue, one that is often not addressed. That issue is one of meaning, purpose, and truth. After all, given proper diagnosis and expert help with needed skills, a person could become a better thief. When assessment is left at the level of technical skills and interests, there is no compelling moral matrix, no redeeming social purpose. I suppose that it is possible to reason that in schools we would not attempt to teach anything that is not morally and socially uplifting, so only good skills would be taught and learned. Well, even if this were the case, there is still an obligation to find out whether students know this for sure.

Of the various strategies detailed in this book, I especially recommend the following in the quest for meaning, purpose, and value: *Search for Meaning* (p. 106), *I Can Teach* (p. 118), *Focus Groups* (p. 131), *Clear and Unclear Windows* (p. 72), *Circle Meeting* (p. 122), and *Thank You* (p. 125). These strategies contain a greater measure of affect, and they can be specifically targeted at matters of personal relevance, group cohesion, honesty in sharing, responsibility, and empowerment. These strategies place emphasis on the following *practical* aspects of assessment integrated with teaching and learning in classroom life:

♦ Understanding and being understood

♦ Language and communication

♦ Relationship of meaning to action

♦ Reality as socially defined and agreed upon

♦ Prudent moral action

If you achieve the outcomes listed above, you will have made great strides toward building an environment where people really try to find purpose and meaning in a group setting. Beyond these good efforts, however, lies an entire realm of empowerment and freedom in the world of assessment. The strategies can take you there, but you must sincerely want to go there with your students. The process takes time and patience. It won't happen overnight. This world includes the following assessment possibilities:

♦ Emphasis on transcendence

♦ Building a climate of openness

♦ Self-reflection as expected practice

♦ Group-reflection as expected practice

♦ True freedom of speech and action

CONCLUSION

What I am saying to you is that there are three worlds of assessment. The first world is *technical*. It deals with *how to*. The technical level is goal directed, feedback-controlled, and mainly behavioral. Many teachers seem to be willing to stop at this level, going no further. The second level is the *practical* level where communication is emphasized along with a sense of others, and teaching and learning as a *social activity*. The teachers who reach this level accomplish remarkable things with their students. And the third level is one of *freedom and empowerment*. This very rare level ought to be the long-term goal to which you aspire. Freedom of speech and action, feelings of empowerment, and an atmosphere of transcendence and esprit de corps are the outcomes.

QUESTIONS FOR DISCUSSION AND REFLECTION

♦ Are there differences between assessment and evaluation? If so, what are they?

♦ How comfortable are you with the idea that students assess your teaching?

♦ How do you use information you have about how well your students have learned? Does it influence your teaching decisions?

REFERENCES AND SUGGESTED READINGS

Ainsworth, L. & Christenson, J. (1998). *Student-generated rubrics: An assessment model to help all students succeed*. White Plains, NY: Dale Seymour Publications.

Campbell, C. & Campbell, B. (1999). *Multiple intelligences and student achievement*. Alexandria, VA: Association for Supervision and Curriculum Development.

Ellis, A. (1991). Evaluation as Problem Solving. *Curriculum in Context, 19* (2), 30–31.

Trice, A. (2000). *A handbook of classroom assessment*. New York: Longman.

What do we mean by results? (Feb. 2000). [Special Issue] *Educational Leadership*.

8

NECESSARY CONDITIONS

> *Freedom of expression is the matrix, the*
> *indispensable condition.*
> Benjamin Nathan Cardozo

It is one thing to talk about reflective thinking, metacognitive strategies, and a search for meaning in teaching and learning. It is yet another thing to carefully identify and meet the conditions necessary for such deeper structures to emerge and become reality in a classroom. In this chapter we will address this important issue because unless these conditions are met you cannot expect much to happen beyond business as usual.

The work of Carl Rogers is helpful to teachers who wish to create a participatory, honest, open, and reflective environment. Rogers described several priorities of classroom life. He made it clear that teachers need to work diligently on the development of these priorities. He never suggested that this is an easy task and, like most things worth doing, it takes time.

A CLIMATE OF TRUST

The first priority is to *develop a climate of trust*. Many children and adolescents have learned not to trust others, especially adults. This is unfortunate but true. You can begin to address this problem through a conscious effort to model "trust" in your classroom. The teacher inevitably sets the tone. As your students experience your trust of them, and as you give them reason to trust you and each other, the atmosphere changes in a positive way, not necessarily miraculously, but it does begin to change. Remember that a lack of trust breeds shame and intolerance, and a trust-filled environment breeds openness and caring.

Trust, like the flu, is contagious. When trust happens, it spreads. As you model it, your students will sense its importance and they will begin to act on it. Actions, as we know, speak loudly. But actions must be supplemented with discussion, with a general raising of consciousness. This is the reflective piece. It raises such questions as, "What does it mean to trust someone?" "What happens when people begin to trust each other?" "How does group work depend upon trust?"

Look ahead: Circle Meetings (p. 122)

PARTICIPATORY DECISION-MAKING

A second priority is to *develop a participatory environment of decision-making*. John Dewey described the school as a miniature democracy. Democracy works best when well-informed citizens share in the processes of deciding. You need to think of your students as citizens who you expect to make thoughtful decisions. The notion of the student who keeps to him/herself, offers little or nothing to the group, but does reasonably good work is inadequate in this context. Active participation in classroom life is crucial.

The sociologist Richard Spady writes that every decision made in an organization (think classroom) should be made at the most primary or basic level possible. If Spady is right, this means that you should turn over most of the decisions to your students just as principals should turn over most decisions to teachers. The reason for this is that there is no other way to establish a participatory environment of decision-making. Those organizations that work best, whether they are businesses, governments, or schools are those that have learned that democracy is not an abstract concept but something you practice daily.

A place to start is with the curriculum itself. How many decisions that you presently make for students could actually be made just as well or better by them? We are not talking about a laissez-faire environment or "anarchy comes to school." You are still responsible for and in charge of the basic structure of the environment, but within that structure choices should abound. We get better at those things we take seriously and practice. As your students are given practice in making decisions, they will get better and better at it, practicing citizenship all the while.

Look ahead: Post It Up (p. 100)

SELF-RESPECT

A third priority is to *help students prize themselves.* On the surface this may seem a rather "me" centered idea or a cult of the ego. Nothing could be farther from the truth. The psychologist Ellen Langer makes a powerful distinction between self-esteem and self-respect. She notes that trouble follows when we attempt to cultivate self-esteem. Self-esteem is an evaluative idea that focuses on what others might think of us. Even people with high self-esteem are caught in an evaluative framework. It is not unusual, for example, for convicted felons to have high self-esteem. Self-respect, on the other hand, means accepting who we are, liking ourselves, and even being aware of our limitations without undue worry. By treating your students with respect, by treating them with dignity whatever their ability, you will make a major contribution to their own sense and acceptance of who they are.

As conditions of respect and self-respect emerge in your classroom, the atmosphere changes. You can feel the change. Students look forward to class, they genuinely want to do their best and to reach out to others to help them do their best. They like themselves and therefore are capable of liking others. This stands in deep contrast to an atmosphere of shame and isolation, where students keep to themselves, don't concern themselves with others, and always are expected to "do their own work."

Look ahead: I Can Teach (p. 118), Clear and Unclear Windows (p. 72), Talk About It (p. 89)

SOCIABLE SCHOLARSHIP AND EMOTIONAL EXCITEMENT

A fourth condition of a reflective classroom is one in which the teacher *models the excitement of intellectual and emotional discovery.* This condition implies two things. First, the teacher must be an enthusiastic learner. Secondly, the teacher must be a relational person. John Dewey noted that it is necessary for teachers to become learners and for learners to become teachers. This role reversal means that young people are counting on you, whether they verbalize it or not, to model the qualities of an enthusiastic, inquiring learner. Anything less than this clearly suggests that they would have to invent the behaviors needed to do serious inquiry. The behaviors required of a good learner are far better caught than taught; in other words, example is more powerful than exhortation. The way to begin the process is to ask yourself the question, "What behaviors best model scholarship in the area(s) in which I teach?"

Let's take an example or two for purposes of illustration. If you teach reading, then one behavior you can start with is to raise your profile as a reader. This means that you must do a great deal of reading, especially books of high quality, and that you must share what you are learning with your students. Tell them about ideas, challenges, characters, themes, descriptions, and so on. By the way, it is eminently worthwhile, as well, to share samples of good word choice and syntax by a gifted writer. Beyond that, you might share how you take notes when you read, especially when you are struck by a profound idea or way of saying something.

If you are teaching science, let the students see some of the "scientist" in you. Tell them about your own visits to museums. Share some of your own scientific interests, whether in the reading you do, hobbies and collections, places you have been, how you observe and record, and some of your specific interests related to scientific topics. It really is as simple as that. Of course, if you have little interest in scientific inquiry apart from teaching it as a school subject, then of course we have a problem meeting this condition.

And if you really want to model an even higher level of intellectual excitement and inquiry, then step outside your discipline(s). This is rarely done and when it does happen, students begin to see a whole world of connections. Here are some examples: the mathematics teacher who talks about his/her visit to an art museum; the music teacher who takes some time to demonstrate the physics of music by teaching students about oscillations, sympathetic vibration, and harmonics; and the primary teacher who tells the students about the wonderful class he/she is taking in order to learn more about teaching.

The other aspect of this necessary condition, the emotional excitement, is admittedly easier for some teachers than for others. But teaching, like any serious profession, is not designed merely to be easy. It has been said that all true learning engages the emotions. People learn best when they *feel* some sense of excitement about what they are doing. This type of excitement comes in many forms. Some teachers are far more outgoing and flamboyant than others. This is not the point. Any form of emotional involvement and discovery will communicate to students. You cannot hide it from them because they will sense it in you.

The attitude is one of "I can't wait to get started on this project." Or, typically, when it's caught by the students it manifests itself in such comments as "Do we have to put away our stuff already?" Please allow me to refer you to the *Go with the Flow* chapter found in this book for help with this idea.

CONCLUSION

The necessary conditions of classroom life that we have addressed here are actually rather simple. But they are significant. If you implement them, you will experience a changed environment, one that is at once more intellectually, socially, and morally satisfying and profound. I said the conditions are simple. Indeed they are, but it takes a great deal of commitment to make them come alive. It also takes time, and you ought not to be discouraged by little setbacks along the way. It is worth the effort. Your classroom will become a place of trust, of participation, of respect for self and others, and a place where the excitement of discovery reigns.

QUESTIONS FOR DISCUSSION AND REFLECTION

♦ To what extent would your students say the necessary conditions are already present in your classroom?

♦ What are some barriers that exist in the real world of schools that could make it difficult to realize the necessary conditions? How can these barriers be overcome?

REFERENCES AND SUGGESTED READINGS

Bandura, A. (1971). *Social learning theory*. New York: General Learning.

Brandt, R. (Ed.). (2000). *Education in a new era*. Alexandria, VA: Association for Supervision and Curriculum Development.

Costa, A. & Garmston, R. (1994). *Cognitive coaching: A foundation for renaissance schools*. Norwood, MA: Christopher-Gordon.

Langer, E. (1998). *The power of mindful learning*. Perseus Press.

Rogers, C. (1969, 1983, 1994). *Freedom to learn*. Columbus, OH: Merrill.

Spady, R. & Bell, C. (1998). *The search for enlightened leadership: Applying new administrative theory*. Olympia, WA: Pan Press.

9

IMPROVED SOCIAL SETTING

We are supposed to be getting trained for society but are taught as if each one of us were going to live a life of contemplation in a solitary cell.

Jean Jacques Rousseau

Entire books have been written on the topics of working together, getting along, social skills, conflict resolution, and team building. A complete discussion of any of those matters is beyond the scope of this book. However, we ought not to minimize the role that social skills play in reflective thinking. They are a fundamental condition. Any teacher who has tried group work only to find that the groups never got to the task at hand simply because they were unable to function socially knows the accompanying sense of frustration. Any student who feels that he/she "did all the work" while other group members tagged along will be reluctant to want to repeat the experience. No wonder so many teachers retreat to the safety of an environment where students work alone seated at their desks in rows. To attempt group work in the absence of reasonably developed social skills is analogous to attempting mathematical problem solving with people who cannot do basic computation.

One of the best sources of help when it comes to developing social skills is the book *Working with Emotional Intelligence* by Daniel Goleman. Goleman points out something that experienced teachers know intuitively, and that is, that young people's social skills are on the decline. He notes that "perhaps the most disturbing piece of data comes from a massive survey of parents and teachers that shows the present generation of children to be more emotionally troubled than the last. On average, children are growing more lonely and depressed, more angry and unruly, more nervous and prone to worry, more impulsive and aggressive." (Goleman, p. 11)

As discouraging as this information is, you and I must remain optimistic that improvements can be made. This is why we teach, after all, because we believe we can improve the academic and social skills of the young people we work with. It is difficult sometimes to know just where to begin a process. Must students already possess the requisite social skills in order to do group problem solving and reflective thinking? Or do such experiences give them the opportunity to learn social skills in a meaningful context? I will opt for the latter. At the same time, however, I wish to be sensitive to those teachers who work with students who have trouble functioning in socially arranged learning environments. And that is why I recommend reading Goleman's book as well as the other references found at the end of this chapter.

Goleman lists five categories of requisite skills needed to work effectively with others in group settings. These skills represent the affective side, or as Goleman labels them, "emotional competence." They are as necessary, perhaps more so, than intellectual competence when it comes to group problem solving and shared experience, whether in school, the workplace, or in other settings. They are worth examining at this point. I suggest that you make them topics of study and discussion with your students.

Goleman divides what he calls "emotional competence" into two broad classifications: (1) personal competence, which includes self-awareness, self-regulation, and motivation; and (2) social competence, which includes empathy and social skills.

Look ahead: Circle Meeting (p. 122), Thank You (p. 125)

PERSONAL COMPETENCE

Self-awareness is defined as "knowing one's internal states, preferences, resources, and intuitions." (Goleman, p. 26) Self-awareness includes *emotional awareness*, that is, the ability to recognize one's emotions and their effects; *accurate self-assessment*, knowing one's strengths and limits; and *self-confidence*, a strong sense of one's self-worth and capabilities.

Self-regulation is the ability to manage "one's internal states, impulses, and resources." (Goleman, p. 26) Self-regulation includes *self-control*, keeping disruptive emotions and impulses in check; *trustworthiness*, maintaining standards of honesty and integrity; *conscientiousness*, taking personal responsibility; *adaptability*, or flexibility in handling change; and *innovation*, becoming comfortable with new ideas, approaches, and information.

Motivation is defined by Goleman (p. 26) as "emotional tendencies that guide or facilitate reaching goals." Motivation includes *achievement drive*, or striving to improve toward excellence; *commitment*, or aligning with group goals; *initiative*, or readiness to act; and *optimism*, that is, persistence in spite of obstacles and setbacks.

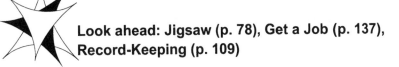

Look ahead: Jigsaw (p. 78), Get a Job (p. 137), Record-Keeping (p. 109)

SOCIAL COMPETENCE

Empathy is defined by Goleman as an "awareness of others' feelings, needs, and concerns." (p. 27) Empathy includes *understanding others*, that is, showing interest in the concerns, feelings, and perspectives of others; *developing others*, or sensing others' needs and bolstering their abilities; and *service orientation*, anticipating, recognizing, and meeting others' needs.

Goleman defines *social skills* as "adeptness at inducing desirable responses in others." (p. 27) Social skills include *influence, communication, conflict management, leadership, cooperation, building bonds, and team capabilities*, all of which are aspects of integrating oneself meaningfully into the group as a supportive, caring member who believes in the group's goals and wants to help fulfill them.

Look ahead: Focus Groups (p. 131), Parents on Board (p. 128)

Those of you who are serious about developing social skills and, what Goleman calls emotional intelligence, need to read his book. You'll come away convinced that emotional intelligence (what we often think of as social skills) is probably more significant than the kinds of intelligence measured by traditional IQ tests.

CONCLUSION

Rousseau wrote that "it is by doing good that we become good." I think his sage advice should be applied to the social context of classrooms. The social skills that I have outlined above represent desirable habits for young people to acquire. But how do they acquire them? The answer is simple, by *doing* them. The evidence shows us that students today are often deficient in social skills. The evidence also shows us that many students are deficient in their mathematics skills. The remedy in either case is the same practice with good coaching and opportunities to reflect on experience.

QUESTIONS FOR DISCUSSION AND REFLECTION ON IMPROVED SOCIAL SETTING

- ◆ Which comes first in your mind: improving the social setting or improving academic achievement?

- ◆ What is the relationship between academic learning and social setting?

REFERENCES AND SUGGESTED READINGS

Freire, P. (1998). *Pedagogy of the heart.* New York: Continuum Publishing Group.

Goleman, D. (1998). *Working with emotional intelligence.* London: Bloomsbury.

Johnson, D.W. & Johnson, F.P. (1999). *Joining together: Group skills.* Boston, MA: Allyn and Bacon.

Salovey, P. & Sluyter, D. (1997). *Emotional development and emotional intelligence: Educational implications.* New York:

10

CONSCIOUSNESS

*The only question is whether we decide to
stand outside the circle or within it.*
Parker Palmer

One purpose of this book is to provide you with ways to raise the level of consciousness, both individual and collective, in your classroom. This is what the 22 strategies, when used faithfully, are designed to accomplish. The thesis I propose is that if you are able to create an environment in which consciousness raising is a clear theme, then you will begin to see positive results in the two areas of classroom life that are most important: *academic achievement* and *quality of life*.

The term "consciousness" is often little understood or misunderstood, so it seems reasonable for us to take some time to explore its meaning and implications in a learning environment. It is widely agreed that consciousness consists of three attributes: language, self-awareness, and theory of mind. All three attributes must be present and encouraged in order for a truly reflective learning environment to emerge and prosper. As you come to value these attributes in yourself and to support them as vital to classroom life, you and your students will experience new dimensions of creativity, initiative, cooperation, caring, and academic excellence.

Does it sound too good to be true? Really, there is nothing magic about it, no mystique, no mystery, just common sense applied in uncommon ways. Let's look at each attribute of consciousness in turn.

LANGUAGE

In his book, *Institutes of Oratory*, written in the first century A.D., the Roman orator and educator Quintilian, proposed the idea that language is our most purely human attribute. Quintilian wisely noted that the school experience should most highly prize language in its various forms of reading, writing, listening, and speaking. As an orator, of course, he placed the primary emphasis on speaking, ironically, something lacking in school environments some twenty centuries later. For reasons known only to a few, school is the one place in life

53

where you are expected *not* to talk most of the time. In the most productive work and leisure environments people tend to talk freely about what they are doing, thinking, or feeling but, with rare exceptions, in school you are expected to be quiet and keep your eyes on your own work. The sadness of this fact is that we have a great deal of research, far too much to refute, that speech and the intellect co-develop, that is, they depend on one another in a symbiotic relationship. Another way of saying this is that speech develops the intellect just as the intellect develops speech.

What this means in practical terms is that you simply must give your students more time to talk to one another about the things they are learning, the school experiences they have, and the ways that they perceive value in what they are learning. Some teachers will ignore this plea because they themselves wish to do all the talking, and others because they prefer the silent atmosphere of a classroom where each student is busy doing his/her "own" work. Still other teachers are reluctant to allow very much student talk because they realize that to do so means that not as much material can be "covered" in such an environment. But this is precisely the point. Not as much material should be covered.

One of the problems in teaching mathematics, for example, is that teachers try to cover too many topics while ignoring the research findings that show that deeper coverage of a few strategic topics results in higher mathematics achievement. (Stevenson, 1994) The coverage game is discredited, in fact it was, years ago, but this is lost on many well-intentioned teachers. A few key topics studied in-depth have far more intellectual potential than many topics studied superficially.

One of the greatest mathematicians and philosophers of the twentieth century, Alfred North Whitehead, admonished teachers in his classic book, *Aims of Education*, not to try to teach too many subjects but to treat a select few in real depth. One key to depth is to allow students to talk about what they are learning, to listen to others talk about it, and to write, read and construct topics at length. This, of course, takes time. But you must be willing to give such time to your students in order to raise the level of consciousness of individuals and of the group as a whole.

SELF-AWARENESS

A second attribute of consciousness is self-awareness, that is, a fully realized sense of one's self, that "I" exist as a being separate from the world around "me," but am at the same time connected to others and the world. It is written in the *Declaration of Independence* that each of us is entitled to life, liberty, and the pursuit of happiness. These stirring words, penned by Thomas Jefferson, underscore our right to a sense of identity apart from others. Each individual exists as a separate entity. As such we have a specific destiny and a right to strive toward self-realization. This may seem all too obvious, but in fact it is a recent idea and one that has yet to take form in much of the world. And as Jefferson and others well knew, the sense of individual identity takes on meaning only in the context of others. This is the beginning of respect, responsibility, and caring.

The work of such psychologists as Abraham Maslow and Carl Rogers has done much to promote the idea of self-realization. Maslow had proposed the idea of a teacher as a "helpful let-be," by which he meant that students should have far more control over their individual academic, social, and moral destinies than we typically give them. Leave them alone so that they can work on things they are interested in, are motivated to learn, and which will enable them to develop a sense of initiative. Rogers, in his book, *Freedom to Learn,* made it clear that the primary issue in classroom life is trust. When teachers begin to trust themselves and to trust their students, a different kind of environment emerges, one in which there is far more freedom accorded the individual to initiate, choose, pursue, and reflect upon his/her learning.

Autonomy is a necessary stage of self-awareness development. The autonomous learner is one who is self-directed, disciplined, responsible, eager to learn, and willing to fulfill his/her obligations to others in a productive learning environment. But how does one achieve autonomy? Like anything else, we get better at those things we practice, especially with expert coaching. The expert coach insists upon practice and knows that giving help is something that needs to be done strategically, not all the time.

Studies in creativity suggest that one way to inhibit its growth in a school setting is to practice surveillance, that is, to monitor every detail of classroom life. For the individual to become just that, an individual, he/she must be given freedom to make mistakes, to learn from the mistakes, to take risks, to advance outlandish ideas, and to pursue his/her own interests. Back to Quintilian for a moment. One of the ideas he promoted and to which a portion of a chapter in this book is dedicated, is the Doctrine of Interest, something that has both attracted and confused educators ever since. Quintilian's idea was that students ought to study those things they are interested in simply because anything else is a waste of time. Of course Quintilian was wise enough to realize that interest on the part of a student is often a function of a good relationship between teacher and students. This is why school subjects are really rather neutral in terms of student like or dislike. The key is who is teaching the subject, how it is taught, and the quality of the experience.

Self-awareness is something that comes fairly early in life, but it must be nurtured in order to fully develop in healthy ways. The best way for a teacher to encourage its growth is to allow freedom of choice within a structured environment of trust where subjects are made appealing and where options exist by which students can meet meaningful learning goals. And how can we be sure whether school learning is meaningful or not? Perhaps we ought to start by asking students to reflect on such matters.

Look ahead: Search for Meaning (p. 106), Percolating (p. 80)

THEORY OF MIND

Theory of mind refers to an awareness of others. This is the realization that others think, have opinions, feelings, ideas, and are conscious beings. At a deeper level lies the realization that one must take this knowledge into account in dealings with others. The implications for the classroom are enormous. Most classrooms are probably smaller than they ought to be and certainly more crowded than we would wish. The time-honored solution to this problem is to have each student occupy his/her own desk area while keeping to him/herself. But this ignores the theory of mind, ensuring that reflective thinking won't happen on any regular basis.

There is a perception that having students work together, to share their thoughts and feelings, meets certain social needs but at the cost of academic learning which is a more personal, individual quest. Widespread as it is, this perception has little basis in reality. The work of such psychologists as Jean Piaget, Noam Chomsky, and Lev Vygotsky, to name only three of many researchers, points in the other direction. Students need to talk about their ideas, to listen to other students, and to work together in situations where task-related conversations occur naturally. And while such experiences do indeed foster social growth, they also foster intellectual growth, and this is especially the case when reflective thought is encouraged.

Cooperative learning, project learning, simulations, group inquiry, learning centers, and other team approaches that invite students to come together in the name of learning are the answer. This is why the extra curriculum is so productive and so attractive. To play on a team, to work together to produce a school newspaper, to put on a play, to be a member of a debate club, all speak to collaboration, to the opportunities to develop theory of mind, to realize that others have something to offer in life. It is certainly no accident that so many new and successful companies encourage a playful, cooperative, creative atmosphere among their employees. And it is vitally important that teachers themselves experience theory of mind through team teaching, collaborative teaching, and even school-wide efforts that involve the entire faculty.

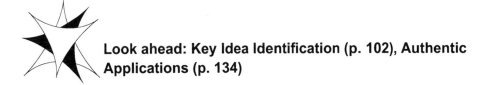

Look ahead: Key Idea Identification (p. 102), Authentic Applications (p. 134)

CONCLUSION

Working and playing together is a necessary but not completely sufficient condition of productive school life. Good experiences cry out for good reflection. For all three attributes of consciousness to come into play, there must be continuous emphasis on reflection, on a search for meaning, on a ferreting out of key ideas, of a sense of what one is learning and how valuable it may or may not be. This is the essence of reflective practice and the way to raise the individual and collective consciousness of students and teachers.

To take seriously the components of consciousness, that is, language, self-awareness, and theory of mind, classrooms will have to be transformed. They must become places where communications skills are practiced daily, where people work together, and where they reflect on the meaning of experience.

QUESTIONS FOR DISCUSSION AND REFLECTION ON CONSCIOUSNESS

♦ Is there some other aspect of consciousness you consider significant?

♦ Describe a time in your own learning when language, self-awareness, and theory of mind appeared to be happening simultaneously.

♦ Which of the three do you think is easiest to establish as a routine? Which is most difficult? Why?

REFERENCES AND SUGGESTED READINGS

Chomsky, N. (1972). *Language and mind*. New York: Harcourt Brace Jovanovich.

Dewey, J. (1922). *Human nature and conduct*. New York: Random House.

Furth, H. (1981). *Piaget and knowledge*. (2nd ed.). Chicago, IL: University of Chicago Press.

Gardner, H. (1991). *The unschooled mind: How children think and how schools should teach*. New York: Basic Books.

Greenspan, S. (1997). *The growth of the mind*. Reading, MA: Addison-Wesley.

Ornstein, R. (1991). *The evolution of consciousness: Of Darwin, Freud, and cranial fire-the origins of the way we think*. New York: Prentice-Hall Press.

Rogers, C. (1969, 1983, 1994). *Freedom to learn*. Columbus, OH: Merrill.

Stevenson, H. (1994). *The learning gap: Why our schools are failing and what we can learn from Japanese and Chinese children*. New York: Touchstone Books.

Vygotsky, L. (1981). *Thought and language*. Cambridge, MA: MIT Press.

Whitehead. A. (1929). *The aims of education*. New York: Macmillan.

11

LIFE SKILLS NEEDED IN THE WORKPLACE

> *This was my life, my life, my career, my brilliant career!*
> Stella Maria Miles Franklin

In his pioneering research done in the 1970s, David McClelland of Harvard identified the crucial differences between the most and least successful people in the world of work. The most successful had three competencies that clearly distinguished them from the least successful: empathy, self-discipline, and initiative.

McClellan's work clearly showed that when these qualities or competencies are present in an individual, the chances are very good indeed that he/she will do well in the world of work. And when they are lacking, even a high level of technical skill is not enough to make a person successful. Technical skills are important, to be sure, but they are not a reasonable substitute for caring about others, for taking responsibility, and for doing the right thing in ambiguous situations.

Further, it is estimated that IQ and academic test results account for less than 25% of job success. Some estimates place it as low as 4%. If we take the lower of the higher figure, then this means that 75% of job success comes from factors other than high test scores. The lower figure would suggest that as much as 96% comes from other factors. Studies also show that the average American IQ has risen 24 points since testing began in 1918, but a careful analysis by Thomas Achenbach and Catherine Howell shows that "emotional intelligence," which is comprised of the three qualities mentioned above and a few other related attributes, is on the decline.

Further studies point to the need for individuals to possess the following qualities in life, whether at work or in other group settings:

- **Team building.** A genuine desire to be a constructive part of group efforts, to build others up, to play whatever role is necessary for the good of the team. (See Jigsaw, p. 78.)

- **Adaptability.** A willingness to accept ambiguity and uncertainty as part of life and to see opportunity in situations where not everything is clearly laid out. (See I Can Teach, p. 118.)

- **Resilience.** The ability to bounce back, to not become easily discouraged when things are difficult, to work with persistence toward meaningful goals. (See Circle Meeting, p. 122.)

- **Optimism.** A sense of hope and a willingness to see the positive aspects of situations in the face of setbacks, a "don't give up and we will win" spirit. (See Optimism, p. .)

These findings suggest that we must search for deeper levels of classroom experience in teaching, learning, and assessment based on: self-awareness, appropriate expression, coherence, trust, initiative, and esprit de corps. All this clearly points to the need for collaborative work, group projects, team efforts, active learning, and an ongoing search for meaning in the things we do. The reason we must strive toward this in classrooms is because a student's career and adult life in general, begins not in the workplace but in childhood and adolescent experience in working with others. As the poet William Wordsworth once wrote, "the child is the father of the man."

The Assessment of American Education study (1991) provides a list of the abilities employers said are most crucial. Only one of the seven clearly represents the cognitive domain. All others relate to desired social/emotional traits:

- Competence in reading, writing, and mathematics.

- Listening and oral communication.

- Adaptability and creative responses to obstacles.

- Self-management, confidence, motivation, goals.

- Group skills, cooperation, teamwork, negotiation.

- Organization, desire to contribute, leadership.

- Learning on the job, learning how to learn.

If all this has some merit, then the question is "what are we doing at school to teach, learn, and assess these attributes?" This is not meant to minimize the need for students to learn the knowledge and skills of reading, mathematics, science, history, geography, and so on. They are and will remain crucial. But just take a moment to reread the seven desired traits listed above. They are not at all an assault on *what* we teach and learn. Rather, they have to do with *how* teaching and learning experiences are organized. They clearly suggest that if we wish to prepare students for the complex world of the future, then we are going to have to organize experiences that require conversation, group work, research skills, and adaptability.

For many teachers and students, this calls for readiness to change the routines of classroom life. In a nutshell, the change demands a more social environment. It means essentially abandoning the model of each student being "taught" in a group and working alone.

QUESTIONS FOR DISCUSSION AND REFLECTION

♦ What would classrooms be like where teachers and students seriously acted on these desired traits?

♦ What are the greatest obstacles to teamwork in school settings? How can they be overcome?

♦ What kinds of classroom experiences do you think best lead to the development of the traits of empathy, self-discipline, and initiative?

REFERENCES AND SUGGESTED READINGS

Achenbach, T. & Howell, C. (1989). Are America's children's problems getting worse? A thirteen-year comparison. *Journal of the American Academy of Child and Adolescent Psychiatry.*

Goleman, D. (1998). *Working with emotional intelligence.* London: Bloomsbury.

McClelland, D. (1973). Testing for competence rather than intelligence. *American Psychologist*, v. 46.

Prochaska, J. et al. (1994). *Changing for good.* New York: Avon.

Sternberg, R. (1996). *Successful intelligence.* New York: Simon and Schuster.

The Harris Education Research Council. (1991). *An Assessment of American Education.* New York: Harris Research.

12

GOING WITH THE FLOW

> I guess I lost track of the time.
> Child returning late from recess.

How many times have students been told by well-intentioned teachers something like, "You may not like this, but you're going to need it in the future." There may be much truth to the assertion that some particular knowledge or skills will likely be needed by most of us in some way. Many painful examples come to mind. But the quote above contains another implied truth: "You may not like this." When need and dislike come together what are the results? It is safe to say that the results are less than when we like to do what we also need. The best educational circumstance is that in which important things are being considered and students want to learn them. Occasionally, this happens in classrooms. More often it happens in the extra curriculum: in athletics, drama, music, art, school newspaper, clubs, and so on. Why is this so?

The psychologist Mihaly Csikszentmihalyi describes a condition he calls "flow." He writes about being "in the flow." He notes that flow occurs most often when there are *clear goals* a person tries to reach, and when there is *unambiguous feedback* as to how well he or she is doing." (p. 179) He writes further: "A second condition that makes flow experiences possible is the *balance between the opportunities for action* in a given situation and *a person's ability to act.*" (p. 181, italics added) The following is Csikszentmihalyi's characterization of the flow experience, that is, of the conditions present when a person is experiencing flow (pp. 178–179):

1. Clear goals: an *objective* is distinctly defined; immediate feedback: one knows instantly how well one is doing (for example, to play the best game we are capable of playing).

2. The *opportunities* for acting are good, and they are matched by a person's ability to act; personal skills are well suited to the challenge.

3. *Action* and *awareness* merge; singleness or one-pointedness of mind.

63

4. *Concentration* on the task at hand; irrelevant stimuli disappear from consciousness. Worries and concerns are temporarily suspended.

5. A sense of potential *control*.

6. Loss of self-consciousness, *transcendence* of ego boundaries, a sense of growth and of being part of some greater entity.

7. *Altered sense of time*, which usually seems to pass faster.

8. The *experience seems worth doing* for its own sake.

Take numbers 4 and 7 from Csikszentmihalyi's list of flow conditions and apply them to your own experience for a moment. *Can you think of some things you like to do that when you do them you find yourself immersed in the task at hand while time seems to pass quickly?*

Look ahead: The Week in Review (p. 76), Write in Down (p. 112)

One couple I asked about this recently said, "Yes, at our weekly bridge game." Another person told me, "When I've got a good mystery novel." A single parent said, "When I'm playing with my kids." For others, perhaps it is tennis, gardening, caring for an infant child, meditating or praying, doing needlepoint, attending the theatre, mountain climbing, cooking, painting, playing the piano, spending time with someone they love, and so on. Artists, musicians, athletes, and performers typically report experiencing flow routinely when asked about it. They love their work or their play, and they will usually tell you that they feel very fortunate to be able to do what they do. In a televised presidential debate in 1992, President George Bush was captured on camera looking at his watch. Apparently this was not a flow experience for him.

Does flow happen in classrooms? The answer is, yes, but not as often as it should happen. *Does it happen in your classroom?* You and your students are the best judge of that. Tell them about flow, explain the idea to them. Tell them about some of your own flow activities or experiences. Ask them about some of theirs. Don't be disappointed if most of the examples come from outside of school. This is typical. The teaching and learning question for you is, "How can I create the conditions for flow to happen in this classroom?" The best single classroom-based answer to this question is found in project learning and other related active, collaborative ways to learn.

If you provide project assignments from which students might choose, especially projects that are collaborative in nature, the chances are pretty good that this step alone will increase the amount of time your students spend in flow activities. Projects have several advantages over traditional school assignments. First of all, they provide for obvious applications of knowledge and skills because students must *use* what they know in order to create the project. Secondly, collaborative projects create the conditions for thinking aloud and sharing ideas, an important metacognitive aspect of learning and assessment so often lacking when students work alone. Thirdly, projects typically are more engaging, they are fun to do. Students like to make things, to display them, and to explain their work to others. Fourthly, projects are practical pursuits. They demand the practical part of us. A product or some kind of tangible outcome, always a goal of the practical, typically results from project involvement. And lastly, collaborative projects provide the kinds of environmental conditions where teamwork is needed and friendships are made.

Another question worthy of consideration for you and your students is "what percent of time spent in school should be time "in the flow." One answer is 100 percent. Another answer is that 100 percent flow time is probably not a realistic outcome. Even certain tasks that we seek out on our own in life have about them a certain measure of the tedious, we just need to do them. But when people feel that what they are doing is meaningful and purposeful, the things that might be nothing more than drudgery take on added significance. We do know this: human beings typically will respond positively to situations where at least 15 percent of the time seems meaningful to them. That's pretty minimal. So, my answer to this question is, "somewhere between 15 and 100 percent ought to be time spent in the flow." And the question of lasting significance is, "How can I get my class closer to 100 percent than to 15 percent?"

CONCLUSION

This chapter on flow and its role in school learning is meant as a bridge to Part II of the book. If things go as I think they will for you, then you will see the obvious transition from a consideration of flow to the 22 strategies that follow. The active, reflective learning emphasized in each of the strategies should give you the means of introducing flow into the classroom experience. An action research project I encourage you to carry out is to record the "flow-related" comments of your students during those times you use the strategies. If you are able to record a substantial number of comments such as, "That was fun!" "Can we do something like this again?" "Can we keep going just a little longer?" then you will have entered the world of flow. This world already exists and is taken for granted in the extra curriculum. Now let's bring it to the classroom.

QUESTIONS FOR DISCUSSION AND REFLECTION ON GOING WITH THE FLOW

♦ What are examples of flow activities in which you engage?

♦ What do you think students would list as examples of school-related flow activities?

♦ Which of the strategies to follow would you predict as the easiest for you to incorporate routinely?

♦ How can a teacher know if his/her students are experiencing flow?

REFERENCES AND SUGGESTED READINGS

Cherniss, C. (1995). *Beyond burnout.* New York: Routledge.

Csikszentmihalyi, M. (1990). *Flow: The psychology of optimal experience.* New York: Harper and Row.

Csikszentmihalyi, M. (1993). *The evolving self: A psychology for the third millennium.* New York: HarperCollins.

Wing, L. (1992, Winter). The interesting questions approach to learning. *Childhood Education,* 78–81.

PART II

REFLECTIVE ASSESSMENT STRATEGIES

> *Teachers, make it your first task to know your students better, for you surely do not know them.*
>
> Jean Jacques Rousseau

SUMMARY OF STRATEGIES

Strategy	*Activity*
I Learned Statements (p. 69)	Statements of personal learning during closure of lesson.
Clear and Unclear Windows (p. 72)	Students sort what is and is not clear at the time.
The Week in Review (p. 76)	Students assess week's activities.
Jigsaw (p. 78)	Home and expert groups master and combine information.
Percolating (p. 80)	Time for reflection.
Pyramid (p. 84)	Rehearsal through gradually increasing group size.

Strategy	*Activity*
Talk About It (p. 89)	Articulate learning out loud to self or another.
Learning Illustrated (p. 92)	Translate understanding into visual representation.
Question Authoring (p. 96)	Students construct questions about the content and skills.
Post It Up (p. 100)	Students post their understanding of the main point.
Key Idea (p. 102)	Identify main concept underlying whole lesson or activity.
Search for Meaning (p. 106)	Try to find the truth in the idea or activity.
Record-keeping (p. 109)	Write down events and ideas to increase awareness of them.
Write It Down (p. 112)	Seven reflective questions for metacognition.
All Things Considered (p. 115)	During closure, find connections.
I Can Teach (p. 118)	Extending understanding through teaching.
Circle Meeting (p. 122)	Structured large group opportunity for individual feedback.
Thank You (p. 125)	Specifically acknowledge the influence of another person.
Parents on Board (p. 128)	Concretely and frequently invite parents to help.
Focus Groups (p. 131)	Small groups discuss classroom experience.
Authentic Applications (p. 134)	Directly connect to real world of work.
Get a Job (p. 137)	Make a real world connection to an actual work experience.

I LEARNED
STATEMENTS

> *The reasonable thing is to learn from those who can teach.*
> Sophocles

PURPOSE

The *I Learned*[*] statement for assessing learning is a quick and efficient way to get a sense of your students' grasp of a lesson or activity. It is beautifully simple, and it achieves two assessment goals at once: (1) each student gives you feedback on what he or she thought was of significance, and (2) the aggregate of the responses informs you to what extent you achieved your teaching goal. Remember, the purpose of school is not teaching; it is learning. Teaching is something one does in order to create opportunities for learning.

PROCEDURE

Here is how the process works. At the conclusion of a class period, with five minutes or so left, ask each student to write down on a sheet of paper, "I learned such and such…" in today's activity or lesson. For example, if you have just taught students how to divide fractions, an *I Learned* statement might read, "I learned that to divide fractions, you invert the divisor and multiply." If you have read students the story of The Three Bears, an *I Learned* statement might read, "I learned that it wasn't right for Goldilocks to break into the Three Bears' cottage." In a lesson on the Lewis and Clark expedition, a student wrote, "I learned that Captain Clark was an excellent map maker." Such simple statements are a reasonable place to begin. As students have practice writing statements, and particularly in the case of older students, the statements will begin to take on greater depth, but all this comes with time.

These three examples come from students who show some basic understanding of significant or main ideas. Of course, not everyone will grasp the main idea, but the point is that even if this is so you are better off knowing that.

---

[*] A description of the *I Learned* statement is found in: Simon, S., Howe, L. & Kirschenbaum, H. (1972). *Values clarification.* New York: Hart Publishing. (The strategy is attributed to Jerry Weinstein.)

It doesn't pay to assume that everyone learned something just because you or I taught it.

In fact, the first time you try *I Learned* statements with your class, don't be surprised if half the papers turned into you are blank. This is nothing to be alarmed about. In most cases, students are never asked what they just learned, so they don't tend to think in those terms. In other words, students are not typically asked to reflect. Also, don't be surprised if many of the papers contain "irrelevant" or "inaccurate" *I Learned* statements. It helps to share insightful *I Learned* statements by students with the class. All that some students need are examples in order for them to grasp the general idea.

I remember having my students write *I Learned* statements following a presentation by a uniformed naval officer who had spoken to the class. One student's response stays in my mind to this day. She wrote, "I learned that they have gold buttons on their coat." Perhaps it could be argued that this was hardly the main idea of the presentation, which was on the topic of careers, but that is what she said she learned.

One of the joys of *I Learned* assessment comes from statements by students who not only grasped the intent of the lesson but who saw in it really good things that you yourself hadn't even considered. In other words, they made connections to some prior knowledge or experience. When students write statements that are insightful and even profound, be sure to read those statements aloud to the class. This will help others to understand the process better.

Sometimes what people need most are good examples to get them started. One of the things you will notice, if you use this technique over time, is that students will get better and better Of course, keep in mind that learning is a complex process and that students may learn things that you feel were not intended or even to the point. Who knows what prior knowledge a given individual might bring to an activity and how it might affect their learning? It serves as a good reminder that even though we might think we are teaching exactly the same thing to all 30 students, that is simply not the case because each individual must construct his or her *own* knowledge. Invariably people will come up with slightly different constructions. You need be concerned only if you are convinced that students are not getting the point at all.

It does matter greatly what is taught when it comes to assessing *I Learned* statements by students. For example, if you are teaching certain skills that you think are crucial, then you do want to be sure that students are grasping those skills. This is what is known as convergent knowledge. However, if you are teaching complex ideas, then it is quite understandable that students might come to varied perspectives on those ideas. You have entered the realm of divergent knowledge. If you are teaching two-place addition, of course, you will hope to receive *I Learned* statements that are related to the skill. Even in such a case, however, the *insights* which students generate in learning this may vary considerably. And if you are teaching something as complex as social skills to your class, expect a wide range of insights and personal applications from students.

OUTCOMES

One of the uses of the *I Learned* statement is diagnostic. If you receive a large number of statements that you feel are inaccurate or misleading you will probably want to try teaching the same material again, probably in a different way. If you receive a mix of statements, you may want to form peer teaching groups in which those who clearly grasp the content or skill are asked to share their knowledge with students who are having trouble with the material.

The aggregate of the *I Learned* responses from a class of students is one of the single best indicators of your success in achieving your objective in a lesson. Taken together, a classroom set of statements forms a kind of mosaic reflecting the quality of the experience. You can control what you teach, but you cannot control what is learned. Sometimes they are basically the same thing, and on other days, well, they are worlds apart.

How often should a teacher use *I Learned* statements? My answer is often, but probably not every day. The thing to keep in mind is that you are attempting to raise the level of consciousness of your students. You are asking them to think about what they are learning. In other words, you are asking them to be reflective, to practice metacognition. Like any technique, the *I Learned* statement can be overused. It is best to use it intermittently, perhaps two or three times a week. In this way, students will have it in the back of their minds that you may use it on any particular occasion, thus helping them to be alert to this possibility and to think about what they are learning just in case they are asked. In time it becomes automatic for them to think that way, in which case you will have achieved a very important educational goal.

VARIATIONS ON THE THEME

I Learned is merely one way to elicit student responses of this nature. Other possibilities include *I Think, I Know, I Feel,* and *I Like* statements. The first two of these are quite close to *I Learned,* but they do give a slightly different slant. The latter two take the matter from the more cognitively oriented perspective to an affective approach. By using *I Feel* or *I Like* statements, students are given the opportunity to express personal preferences, and you are afforded the opportunity to better understand how they feel about things. Student feelings are an extremely important educational indicator. When students like what they are doing and when they have good feelings about school activities, they are much more likely to become deeply involved, more persistent in their attempts to learn and more responsive to your leadership.

CLEAR AND UNCLEAR WINDOWS

"Do you suppose," the Walrus said,
"that they could get it clear?"
Lewis Carroll

PURPOSE

Have you ever found yourself walking down the school hallway when a student wearing glasses comes running along and you ask him to stop for a second while you look at his glasses? Chances are they were smudged, dirty, and so on. You say something like, "Could I see your glasses for a second?" You patiently clean them and give them back, saying, "Better?" The student says, "Yes," and runs off on his way somewhere. You say to yourself, "I don't know how he can even see where he's going." The point is that he couldn't, not very well anyway, and you made things clearer. It's a metaphor for what good teachers do all the time; *they make things clearer.*

Dirty glasses and dirty windows are pretty obvious to us. Our first impulse as adults is to clean them, to make them clear so that people can see out of them. We are not surprised when a student's *glasses* are not clear, even if they were clear that morning when the student left home. Why should we be surprised when their understanding of something we just taught is not clear? So much of what is taught is not clearly learned. And I think you know by now that one of the fixed ideas, one of the familiar refrains, of this book is that school is not really about teaching; it is about learning.

PROCEDURE

The *Clear and Unclear Windows* assessment technique is very simple and straightforward. At the end of an assignment or of a significant chunk of learning that may have taken place over several days, you ask students to draw a vertical line on a sheet of paper and to title one half of the paper *Clear* and the other half *Unclear*. On the half titled *Clear*, a student is asked to list those things he/she understands. On the other half, the student lists those things that are not clear or that are poorly understood.

Of course, this represents self-reporting. The fact that a student says he/she understands something clearly does not guarantee that he/she does. However, it is a good place to start. And inevitably if someone tells you they don't understand something or that it is unclear to them, this is surely the case.

This particular assessment procedure assumes a great deal of trust between teacher and students. Trust lays the groundwork for effective communication and is essential to its success. No student wants to tell a teacher that something was too difficult if the result is punishment or a sense of being considered lazy or slow to learn. But finally, wouldn't you rather know than not? Nothing is gained by pretending that everyone learned yesterday's lesson, and now we are ready to proceed on to today's if that is not in fact the case. When a student fails to understand a key idea or skill, especially in courses built on sequential knowledge, then that student ends up paying compound interest on the learning deficit when it comes to learning the next idea or skill. Discouragement sets in, and the will to learn diminishes. This is the beginning of disaster for that student's future hopes.

Those students who indicated that they *do* understand clearly are in a good position to help you with some strategic remediation. The psychologist Jean Piaget once noted that there are times when it is more efficient to have students teach each other because the linguistic compatibility within the peer group makes communication less complex and dense. Remember, you have an adult understanding of the subject matter as well as an adult vocabulary, and sometimes this can get in the way.

OUTCOMES

Asking students to list things that are clear to them and things that are not clear to them forces them to think about (1) what they are learning well, and (2) where the problems lie. Self-diagnosis is a valuable skill because it enables the learner as well as those entrusted to help the learner to know where to start. Sometimes just knowing where to start is the key to unlocking deeper learning. For example, consider this statement written by a student in a science class:

> It isn't clear to me how hydrogen and oxygen go together to make water. How can two gases be put together to make a liquid? I just don't get it.

This same student had written on the clear side of the sheet of paper:

> I know that hydrogen and oxygen combine to make water. I know that two atoms of hydrogen are needed and one atom of oxygen, that's why it is H2O.

HYDROGEN AND OXYGEN COMBINE TO MAKE WATER

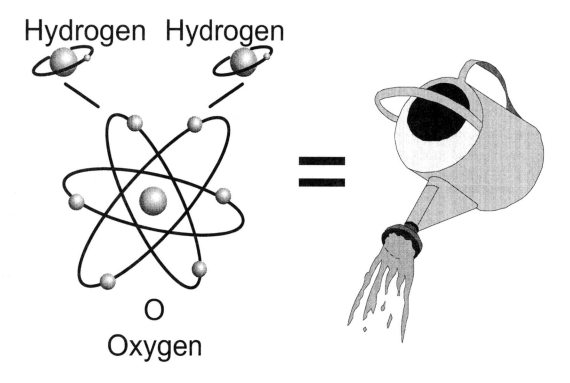

Hydrogen Hydrogen

=

O

Oxygen

In many cases learning is assumed because superficial knowledge is in place. That is exactly the situation this student is in. The student knows the words to describe water as a product of hydrogen and oxygen in combination, but the student has no clue as to how the process actually works. Maybe the teacher "covered" the process in class or maybe not, but at least one student has indicated a lack of scientific understanding that the teacher can no doubt easily clear up in the following class period. It has been noted that even higher achieving students in advanced science classes more often than not give medieval answers to such scientific questions as how the seasons change, how gravity works, and what causes night and day. *Clear and Unclear Windows* does at least give students the opportunity to let you know about such things.

As students become more adept at writing *Clear and Unclear Windows*, they will help you take your teaching to deeper levels of knowledge and insight. This process is obviously useful with lower achieving students who are struggling to keep up, but it is equally useful with higher achievers, many of whom will frankly confess they don't understand the subject matter very deeply and are merely good at parroting back superficial information on tests and in discussions.

Because the application of this technique, like that of others mentioned in these pages, is strategic, it is not necessary that you use it every day. In fact, one approach is to allow students to turn *Clear and Unclear Windows* statements in to you whenever they would like to. However, I do suggest that you conduct this as an activity with the class several times a month in order to ensure adequate opportunity for each one of your students to let you know just what is clear and unclear to them.

THE WEEK IN REVIEW

> *If I am to speak for ten minutes, I need a*
> *week for preparation.*
> President Woodrow Wilson

PURPOSE

The Week in Review (TWR) is a collaborative activity in which students take an evaluative perspective on the classroom events and activities of the past several days. The idea of *TWR* is similar to that of the television program *Washington Week in Review,* in which several talking heads sit together, each offering his/her perspective on the significant national and international events of the week. The heart of the matter is a discussion of the implications and meaning of those events. The difference is that your students will discuss the major happenings of the week in the classroom or at school in general in some cases, as they see them.

PROCEDURE

TWR typically takes about 30 minutes and is best conducted on a Friday. In order to maximize participation, it is advantageous to ask each student to take five minutes or so to work alone, making a list of what he/she thinks were the three or four most significant ideas, activities, experiences, and so on, of the week. By bringing a written list a student is far more likely to contribute to discussion because he or she has been afforded an opportunity to give the matter some prior thought. This also provides a level of structure often missing in small student group interaction.

Each member of the group is given the opportunity to share his/her ideas, and then the discussion begins. The challenge for each group is to come to some agreement on the significant events of the week and to prepare a list to be reported to the class and turned in to you. In a typical classroom, this means that 8 to 10 group lists will be generated. This will give you the luxury of having a large number of thoughtful perspectives on what your class thinks was significant. Procedures such as *TWR* can go a long way in reducing the gap between what important things the teacher thinks he/she is teaching and what important things the students think they are learning. This represents the pursuit of the practical in classroom life; it is a search for understanding.

The ideal group size for this activity is three, possibly four students. This provides multiple perspectives while allowing each group member a chance to share. Research in small group interaction* has shown consistently that for purposes of participation by all members, the optimum group sizes are two, three, or at most, four. When groups are larger than this, certain members withdraw from active participation, and one or two members will dominate. If you use a group size of four, I suggest that you assign one group member the role of moderator, whose task it is to be sure that the other three members are each invited to contribute to the discussion.

Outcomes

TWR serves several purposes. First of all, students are encouraged to reflect on what they have done in the past several days and on the significance of the activities, and so on, in which they have participated. What was important? What were some key ideas? What have we learned that has some significance? What was enjoyable? What could have been improved? This is the beginning of the search for meaning.

Secondly, your students' sense of what was meaningful is something for you to compare with your own sense of what you tried to accomplish this week. What were the key ideas you tried to get across? What did you think was significant about the activities when you planned for them? To what extent did you achieve your objectives? What do *you* think were the highlights of the week? And thirdly, the student review gives you a good place to begin on the following Monday by using it to connect what went before to where you think things ought to be going. One of the most persistent problems in teaching and learning is the lack of connectedness between and among lessons. Too often, each lesson appears to be an island of instruction, an event unto itself. *TWR* gives you and your students a port of entry for the new week based on last week's learning. In fact, a good way to start Monday morning is by summarizing what the students had to say in their analyses.

---

*   Ellis, Arthur K. (1998). *Teaching and learning elementary social studies.* (6th ed.). Boston: Allyn and Bacon, p. 358.

JIGSAW

> *We must try to trust one another. Stay and cooperate.*
> Jomo Kenyatta

PURPOSE

The jigsaw strategy, developed by Elliot Aronson, is an interesting combination of cooperative learning with an individualistic goal structure. The idea of jigsaw is that each student in a cooperative learning group of, say, three students is responsible for peer teaching his/her companions a portion of the material that they all need to learn. Thus each student "teaches" one-third of the information, skills, or whatever, and is "taught" two-thirds of the content. It is important that students do their best to teach their compatriots well because all the members of a group are depending on each other. This truly creates a "we're in this together" mentality.

PROCEDURE

When a jigsaw group of students is assembled, it is crucial that each member has something tangible to contribute. This means preparation, an important step in any problem solving process. I recommend that in most cases, you require that students write down clear notes or points that they wish to cover during the time the group meets. Any materials or illustrations should also be assembled in advance. This way, when the group comes together, the time is spent productively. Because you will typically have three students in a group, you will have to make it clear that each person should be given equal time to present. Of course, you should allow a few minutes for each group to converse informally, a sort of "warm up" time, and you should allow time at the conclusion of the presentations for the group to do some reflective thinking about what they have learned.

There is an intermediate step that can greatly contribute to the success of the *Jigsaw* strategy. Let us say for the sake of example that the topic is tidal action. Step One is for each student to prepare his/her part of the presentation to the group. Step Three is for the groups to come together and teach each other so that all important points are covered. But keep in mind that in a class of 30 students this means that three potential groups of 10 students each studied the same part of the lesson. So, Step Two brings students together (perhaps in groups of five to keep things manageable) who have studied the same thing. They are able to check with each other for accuracy, ideas, procedures, and so on. This intermediate step helps to ensure more accurate presentations, and it gives each student a kind of rehearsal prior to his/her presentation. So, to return to our topic of tidal action, the students who studied causes will meet together briefly, as will those who studied effects, and as will those who studied areas of extreme tides. When that step is completed, students are ready to join their jigsaw groups.

OUTCOMES

I've included *Jigsaw* among our strategies for bringing teaching, learning and assessment together because I'm convinced that peer teaching is one of the best ways for students to learn and to become conscious of what they are learning. I mentioned earlier Jean Piaget's conclusion that children are more effective than most adults realize in teaching each other, especially if teachers provide some structure and support. This is so, he claimed, because of a language issue, namely that greater syntactic compatibility is found within the peer group than exists when, for example, adults talk to children.

What this means in simple terms is that adult language is far more complex than children's language; therefore, a child or adolescent talking to peers does not take linguistic shortcuts, use sophisticated terminology, or assume years of experience. John Dewey once noted that one of the biggest problems in teaching is the false assumption by teachers, of experience on the part of students. All of this in no way diminishes the importance of your role as a teacher; it does, however, shift the center of gravity from you to the students, making your job one of organizer and facilitator of learning rather than lecturer or presenter.

EXAMPLE: THE AMERICAN REVOLUTION

Three events that took place leading up to the American Revolution were: The Boston Tea Party, The Battle of Lexington, and Paul Revere's ride. Each student group of three is assigned the responsibility of learning about them. Using the *Jigsaw* strategy, each student within a group takes one of the events and studies it thoroughly.

After they have had an opportunity to study their events and to prepare their ideas, the "Tea Party," "Lexington," and "Revere" groups each meet together to compare notes. Then the *Jigsaw* groups are convened, and students take turns teaching their peers. You will need to coach your students in techniques for making the information they present interesting, significant, and involving. With practice, the students will improve their teaching, especially if they have learned a variety of teaching strategies that you have modeled and discussed reflectively with them.

PERCOLATING

> *My plans require time and distance.*
> Marcus Whitman

PURPOSE

Studies done years ago by Mary Budd Rowe and others showed conclusively that the amount of time following questions asked of students by teachers is typically in the range of less than one second. What Rowe showed us with her insightful research is that teachers, even those who pose probing questions, unwittingly tend to reward impulsivity rather than reflection.

I say unwittingly because no teacher would tell you that he/she is trying to get the students to answer as quickly as possible without really thinking about their answers. Reflective thinking is a recurrent theme of this book and I want to do whatever I can to convince you how necessary it is to productive classroom life, whether academic or social/moral.

The *Percolating* strategy should help you through this problem by giving you a concrete means of asking reflective questions that require reflective answers. Reflection takes time, and it takes consideration. Often it involves digging beneath the surface, going beyond the obvious, and making sure of one's ideas before expressing them.

PROCEDURE

Here is how *Percolating* works. You pose a problem or question, and you tell the class you do not want an immediate answer. You want students to take some time before answering, and you want them to do some research and reflection along the way.

For example, one approach to *Percolating* is to pose the "Question of the Week." The question of the week must be a probing question, one that goes beyond a "right" answer. The question goes up on the board or is posted in a prominent place in the room on Monday morning, and the follow-up discussion will be held on Thursday or Friday. This gives students time to do some reading, to discuss the matter with each other, to talk to their parents, to find expert opinions, and so on. It is important that students write down their thoughts in order to bring focus and discipline to the discussion. Of course, with younger learners, the writing portion may have to be deleted

Let me return to an example I used in the *Clear and Unclear Windows* strategy:

> *Water is composed of two elements, hydrogen, and oxygen. What is the process by which these two gases combine to form a liquid substance?*

A teacher posed the question and students were encouraged to look for the answer in science texts, to talk to science teachers, to consult with scientists; in other words, to do whatever they could to determine the answer. They were also encouraged to consider showing their answers in as many different ways as they could, for example, using drawings, flow charts, models, demonstration, writing, or whatever. The interesting comment that came up recurrently during the investigation was that most of the students knew that water = H_2O, but they had little or no idea of how these two elements actually come together to form water.

Another teacher posed the question:

> *What could we do to get our school more involved in our community and our community more involved in our school?*

There is an obvious difference between this question and the "water" question. The "water" question has a definite, determinable answer, and the "involvement" question is open to a wide variety of answers, which might well differ depending upon local context. However, they are both alike in that they take time to answer. Even in the case of the "water" question where perhaps one or two students already know the answer, the point is that we want all our students to come to terms with how the world of nature operates. Therefore, we do not want a quick response.

An English teacher posed the following question:

> *How are the short stories of Washington Irving different from and/or like those of Ernest Hemingway?*

This question sent students scrambling to do some reading as well as to attempt to get some "expert" opinion. The discussion that followed later in the week was rich with examples from the stories of each author as students tried to make their case.

OUTCOMES

Questions or problems that require some *Percolating* should generally relate to the context of the ideas, skills, knowledge, and values being studied by the class. By making such connections, a teacher builds in a reflective component to the course of study. Any subject worth studying has tremendous potential for probing questions and problems that require reflective thought. One test of the value of the subject matter you are teaching is its potential to raise such questions and problems.

You need to develop the questions and problems most suited to the topics you teach. However, you do not need to do it alone. This is an excellent discussion topic for a teaching team because it forces each of you to think deeper than the surface considerations. And don't overlook the creative potential of your students. They are perfectly capable of thinking up probing questions and reflective problems. I encourage you to have a box on your desk labeled *Percolating* into which students are invited to place their ideas for questions and problems.

THALES THE GEOMETER

The ancient Greek mathematician and philosopher Thales (6th Century B.C.) Once journeyed to Egypt where it is said he used his knowledge of geometry to measure the height of the Great Pyramid and other structures. He also is said to have been able to calculate the distance from shore to nearby ships at sea.

Thales was able to calculate the height of the Great Pyramid or any other object using simple methods. All he needed was sunshine to cast shadows and a knowledge of his own height.

The question for students is:

> With this much information, do you think you can calculate the height of the flagpole or some other structure at your school?

This problem can be posed as a *Percolating* question to be put on the board on Monday morning with discussion and solutions presented later in the week. Or, it can be posed as a *Think Aloud* problem for students to solve in pairs.

Here is how Thales is said to have solved the problem. He stood near the Great Pyramid and waited until his own shadow was exactly the same length as he was tall. For example, if someone is 5 feet tall and has a 5-foot shadow, then it is merely a matter of measuring the length of the shadow of the Great Pyramid because that is how tall the Pyramid is. Of course, you wouldn't have to wait until your own shadow is exactly your height. You could use proportions. For example, if your shadow is half your height, then the structure whose height you are calculating would also have a shadow half its height.

PYRAMID
DISCUSSION

> *Discussions tend to improve when people*
> *get a chance to talk.*
> Annette L. Clemens

PURPOSE

A class discussion has two main purposes: (1) to exchange ideas and clarify thinking through public discourse, and (2) to maximize student participation in the exchange. Thus a good discussion is both active and reflective.

The teacher's role is that of skillful questioner and guide. It is a bit of an art form in reality. To ask penetrating questions, to stay on topic, and to invite as many students as possible into a discussion is not an easy task. In a room with 30 students, the mathematics are against you going in. Let's say that a discussion lasts 40 minutes, which would be against the odds, but for the sake of example we can use such a length to illustrate the fact that this leaves about 10 minutes for teacher talk and about 1 minute per student assuming everyone contributes.

The problem is compounded by the reality that not every student speaks up during class discussion. This is so for different reasons such as reluctance to speak in front of a group, uncertainty as to what one ought to say, and even the age-old inability to get one's two-cents worth in when so many people want the floor. This is why most class discussions are actually discussions between the teacher and three or four students while most of the class sits by. This doesn't necessarily mean the silent majority are not learning, but a major goal of discussion is defeated when people don't talk.

PROCEDURE

I wish to propose a remedy in the form of the *Pyramid Discussion*. The pyramid approach maximizes student talk while meeting the goal of having everyone hear what needs to be said. Here is how it works.

The teacher (or perhaps in time, the students themselves) prepares several key questions on the topic at hand. You do not need very many questions, perhaps two or three, but they should be strategic in that they get to the heart of the matter. The questions are placed on the board, given out on paper, or otherwise made available to every student. Each student is given a few minutes to write down his/her thoughts in answer to the questions. It is important to have students commit their ideas in writing if possible. Of course, with younger students the entire procedure is carried out orally.

When they have had an opportunity to think through their ideas alone, students are placed in discussion pairs. Dyads (groups of two) maximize each person's opportunity to speak to an "audience," however small. This discussion should take about five minutes or so as students share their ideas with a partner. This portion of the discussion is the least threatening to those students who are initially reluctant to share their thoughts with an entire class. It is easy for teachers to overlook how difficult this is for many students.

XX   XX   XX   XX

Now we begin a geometric expansion of the discussion groups. Two pairs are put together to form groups of four.

XXXX   XXXX

After students have had an opportunity to share in a group of this size, we move to groups of 8, 16, and finally to full class size:

XXXXXXXX

The teacher's role up until the group reaches full class size is to move around the room, monitoring the groups, providing assistance when or where it is needed.

By the time we reach full class size, every student will have had ample opportunity to think about and discuss the questions, thus providing several rehearsals for the discussion in which the teacher leads the entire class. This repeated practice underscores the fact that the discussion questions must be thoughtful, probing questions, ones that are worth going over several times. If we are serious about sustained, reflective thought, this process will help us meet that goal.

OUTCOMES

I think if you try this approach to class discussion you will find highly increased levels of student involvement and far more thoughtful answers to questions as well. The difference between reflective and impulsive answers is lost on some teachers. Thoughtful answers to difficult questions take time and practice. The reward should be not to the quick but to the thoughtful. It takes time to build a reflective environment, one in which teachers and students search for meaning in depth. By using the pyramid, you maximize the potential for everyone to take part in reflective discourse. Everybody gets a piece of the action. The "Boxes in the Balance" problem that follows is ideal for promoting a pyramid strategy.

THE BOXES IN THE BALANCE PROBLEM

In this problem, students are given the accompanying illustration and asked to solve the three problems, giving reasons for their answers. This first step is to be carried out individually.

The second step is for students to share their reasoning with a parent or someone else at home.

The following day, students are asked to share their "teaching experience" with other students in groups of three.

The pictures below show the results when some boxes are placed on a balance.

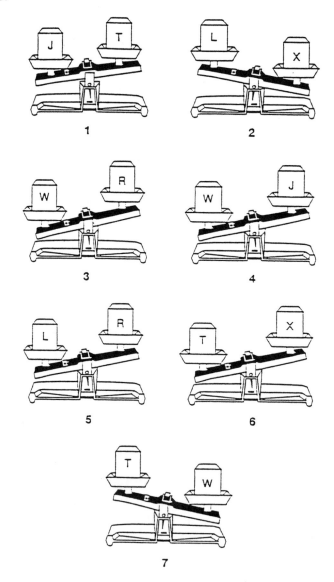

Source: Washington State Department of Education (2000), Olympia, Washington.

Do the following:

◆ Name 2 boxes that are heavier than Box X. Write the number of the picture or pictures you used to find each of your answers.

| |
| |
| |

◆ Tell whether Box R is lighter or heavier than Box X. Write the number of the picture or pictures you used to find your answer.

| |
| |
| |

◆ List the 6 boxes in order from heaviest to lightest.

(1)	(4)
(2)	(5)
(3)	(6)

General Scoring Criteria for Extended-Response Mathematical Reasoning Items

4 points — Student's response show effective interpretations, comparisons, or contrasts of information from sources; effective use of examples, models, facts, patterns, or relationships to validate and support reasoning; insightful conjectures and inferences; or systematic and successful evaluation of effectiveness of procedures and results; with effective support for arguments and results.

3 points — Students's response shows partially effective interpretations, comparisons, or contrasts of information from sources; use of examples, models, facts, patterns, or relationships to validate and support reasoning; expected conjectures and inferences; or mostly successful evaluation of effectiveness of procedures and results; with acceptable support for arguments and results.

2 points — Student's response shows routine interpretations, comparisons, or contrasts of information from sources; examples, models, facts, patterns, or relationships which partially validate and support reasoning; naive conjectures and inferences; or partial evaluation effectiveness of procedures and results with partial support for arguments and results.

1 points — Student's response shows an attempt to interpret, compare, or contrast information from sources; examples, models, facts, patterns, or relationships may not be included to validate or support reasoning; naive conjectures and inferences; or attention to wrong information or persistence with faulty strategy when evaluation effectiveness of procedures and results.

0 points — Student's response shows very little or no evidence of reasoning or the prompt may simply be recopied, or may indicate "I don't know" or a question mark (?).

TALK ABOUT IT

> *The little girl had the making of a poet in her who, being*
> *told to be sure of her meaning before she spoke, said,*
> *"How can I know what I think 'til I see what I say?"*
> Graham Wallas

PURPOSE

The *Talk About It* strategy is designed to accomplish three primary goals. The goals are: (1) creating a self-feedback mechanism; (2) testing one's ideas in public; and (3) making thought processes more intentionally deliberate. The achievement by students of these three goals will go a long way toward creating a reflective perspective in problem solving and other higher-order learning experiences.

Perhaps you've watched a tennis match on television and noticed that some of the players seem to have a habit of talking to themselves. The legendary tennis champion, John McEnroe, was particularly noted for practicing this behavior on the court in front of a stadium full of spectators. Psychologists commenting on McEnroe's self-talk tended to agree that he was doing something very useful. McEnroe's self-talk (often he would berate himself) served as a means of focusing his attention, helping him to concentrate under difficult conditions, and reminding him after all why he was out there, which was to play his best.

Students trying to solve problems can benefit from this strategy. It really seems to help to talk to oneself in the course of problem solving. It does focus attention on the problem. It does help with concentration. Of course, a classroom might tend to become a trifle noisy if all students were talking their way through mathematics problems, but there is no reason why they cannot do this as part of their homework. Self-talk is one form of this strategy. Thinking aloud with a partner is another.

PROCEDURE

A simple technique is to require students to talk to themselves as they solve at least one of the problems or assignments given to them as homework. This creates a feedback mechanism that may be the one thing lacking in the student's approach to his/her work. You can set the stage for a pretty good class discussion by asking students how thinking aloud (either through self-talk or with a partner) changes how they think through a problem.

A second benefit afforded the learner by the *Talk About It* strategy is that which derives from expressing our views to someone else. It is often the case that when our thinking goes astray we are the last to know because everything seems fine according to our own interior logic. By keeping our thoughts to ourselves, we lose the benefit of the outside perspective needed to test the validity of our ideas. If I am trying to solve a problem or understand a procedure or situation, I have to think about what to do as well as do it.

But what if my reasoning is obviously (to others) faulty? This is what critics are for, to help us know what we're doing right and possibly wrong. So, if I tell you how I'm solving a problem, I have to use my logic again, which is all to the good, but more than that, I am given the opportunity to test my logic in a kind of open-air marketplace. And, of course, if you are my partner, I get the added benefit of listening to you tell me how you solved the problem.

OUTCOMES

The benefit is actually double: (1) saying out loud how I'm thinking forces me to be clear to myself and others, and (2) the process allows you to ask me questions, to challenge my assumptions, and to try to understand me. Thus the talker gains whether he/she was using valid reasoning or not because the process has been "inspected."

Related to these two outcomes is a third; talking about something you're thinking about forces you to slow down, to be more deliberate. There is good evidence to show that average and below average learners in particular tend to skip steps in solving problems. In their hurry to accomplish a task, they leave out important procedures that end up making all the difference in the world. The ancient Greek storyteller, Aesop, reminds us in the tale of *The Tortoise and the Hare* that the race is not necessarily won by the swift, but by the sure.

The student who reads a story quickly does not necessarily understand what he/she has read better than the more deliberate reader. A good artist or poet is seldom judged by how quickly they painted a picture or wrote a verse. A good craftsman takes his/her time to do a job well. The effect of slowing down learning is greatly undervalued by most teachers. And when you talk about what you're thinking, it slows you down. This is a first step toward quality.

THINKING ALOUD ACTIVITY

The Counting Triangles Activity works as follows:

1. Each student is given a copy of the triangles diagram and asked to figure out the number of triangles.

2. Students meet in pairs to share their answers, but more importantly to share with their partner *how* they went about solving the problem.

3. Students report back to the class as a whole in order to find out how many different strategies were used.

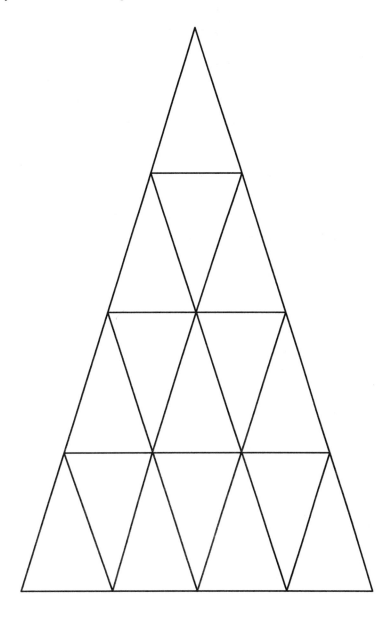

LEARNING
ILLUSTRATED

> *Well, back to the old drawing board.*
> Peter Arno

PURPOSE

Years ago there was a comic book series known as *Classics Illustrated*. The series included the works of such notable writers as Shakespeare, Sir Walter Scott, Mark Twain, Leo Tolstoy, Jules Verne, Mary Shelly, and others. As a child, I read most of them. I thought, and so did my teachers, that I was well acquainted with the great books of Western literature. After all, these comic books had everything you generally needed to take part in a discussion or to pass a school exam: plot, setting, main characters, and so on. And because they were largely pictorial with a few key utterances thrown in, I even "knew" such things as how people dressed, what the architecture looked like, and a sense of geographic setting. The words that were spoken by the characters were usually quotable and memorable because most of the words from the real books were missing. It was the triumph of illustration over print. In time even I learned that there is more to literature than this. But it was a place to start, and it did meet a need that led to the desire in time to read the real books.

Have you ever asked a child to explain something to you and the child replies, "Well, I know but I can't explain it." The chances are pretty good that the child *does* know and could explain it although not perhaps in words. The problem for children, especially younger children, is putting what they know into words. But they do like to draw.

Let's face it, you don't have to be able to explain something orally or especially in writing to know how to do it. Many young children know how to tie their shoes, a difficult skill, but could not write a paragraph explaining how they do it. In fact, there is often little relationship between mastery of a skill and the ability to explain it. Often, outstanding athletes are not particularly adept at analyzing and communicating their world-class skills. But few people would be foolish enough to say those athletes don't know what they're doing on the basketball court, skating rink, and so on.

I recall giving a mapmaking assignment to a class of university students. They were to go out into the environment around the university and observe, record, and map a certain portion of the landscape. When the students turned their products in to me, I was surprised that among the best maps were those turned in by students who were not necessarily anywhere near the "top" of the class. Of course, I should have known that we use biased information, heavily biased toward reading and writing skills, to determine our ideas of who the "top" students are.

PROCEDURE

One of the most natural modes of childhood expression is that of drawing a picture. Most children love to draw, and in most cases they have not yet formed an idea of whether they are "good" at drawing. They simply enjoy this medium of showing what they know, of expressing their thoughts and feelings. They have not acquired the verbal skills of later years, so they depend on this method of expression. As time goes by, teachers rely more and more on writing skills as a way of knowing what students know and feel, and less and less on student pictorial representation. This is unfortunate.

Anyone who has visited a good art museum can tell you that iconic expression is among the most powerful modes of conveying an idea, mood, or sense of place. In most books, words are merely supplemented by pictures, but in an art exhibit, pictures are supplemented by a few words of explanation. There is, of course, the old saying that one picture is worth a thousand words. One of the shortcomings of the Lewis and Clark journey of discovery is that President Thomas Jefferson did not make provision for a sketch artist to accompany the expedition. Just imagine the pictorial treasures we would have today: illustrations of Native Americans, the wilderness landscape of the West, the many animals and plants seen along the way, the travelers themselves, and so on.

STUDENT'S SKETCH OF ARTIFACT

Without doubt, the school assessment tradition is heavily biased toward letters and numbers. Why wouldn't it be? School assignments are heavily biased toward letters and numbers. This is not meant as a complete indictment of the school experience. But I do wish to go on record as saying that far too much of the assessment protocol is weighted toward reading, writing, and numbers. Academics always have been and probably always will be oriented primarily toward symbolic learning, but we are becoming increasingly more aware of the importance of other learning modes and means of expression.

I mentioned earlier in the chapter on Ways to Learn, that the psychologist Jerome Bruner[*] has argued for balance in the school curriculum among the types of teaching and learning that he calls symbolic, iconic, and enactive. His point, a familiar one, is that symbolic learning plays far too dominant a role in teaching and learning, and that even our emphasis on symbols (words, numbers) could be qualitatively improved through greater emphasis on visual and active learning. Iconic learning involves images, and enactive learning involves "hands-on" experience. It is on iconic learning, the mode represented so well in *Classics Illustrated*, that I wish to focus our attention here.

Learning Illustrated calls on students to use essentially nonverbal means to show that they have learned a concept, skill, procedure, or content. The procedure involves sketches, drawings, maps, flow charts, diagrams, graphs, or any other iconic means of demonstrating knowledge. For example, if your class has been studying meteorology, the science of weather and climate, then students might select a concept such as cloud types to illustrate, making drawings of cumulus, stratus, cirrus, and other cloud formations. If students in an English class have been studying *The Adventures of Tom Sawyer*, then a task might be to make a map of the story or to draw a picture of how they think one of the scenes from the book should look.

An example of an extended activity is to have each student select a scene in the local environment and draw, sketch, map, or otherwise illustrate it throughout the course of the day, from morning until evening. The changes in light, shadow, and color will come to life as the observer/recorder begins to notice these subtleties more closely under varied conditions.

Perhaps the most innovative twist on *Learning Illustrated* is to ask students at the end of a lesson to draw a picture, make a flow chart, construct a diagram, create a map, or complete some other graphic rendering of the lesson. This affords them the opportunity to reconstruct the lesson in a completely novel way. It asks them to step outside the normal boundaries of thought and expression and to employ a metacognitive strategy as they reflect back on what was taught and learned.

---

[*]   Bruner, J. (1996). *The Culture of Education*. Cambridge: Harvard University Press.

OUTCOMES

There is little new in this idea. However, when such a task as illustrating something one has learned is placed within the matrix of a range of reflective strategies as one of a number of meaningful ways to advance student learning, then *Learning Illustrated* plays a role in providing variety and choice. Remember, the more ways you have of gaining knowledge of student learning, the better informed you will be, and therefore the better informed your constituencies (students, parents) will be. An additional outcome is that of providing a much needed nonverbal means for students to show themselves and others that they are indeed leaning.

QUESTION AUTHORING

> *I heard you asking questions…: Who killed the porkchops?*
> *What price bananas? Are you my angel?*
> Allen Ginsberg

PURPOSE

It is not at all unusual for students to be asked to answer a set of questions about some material they have read, a film they have seen, or a demonstration/presentation which they have attended or participated in. Mathematics assignments are typically wholly that: "Answer all the odd numbered problems on page 62 for tomorrow." In fact, answering someone else's questions is the most common type of assignment and homework given by teachers.

What would happen in school if students got to ask the questions? The *Question Authoring* strategy turns the assignment around. Students pose the questions. They assume ownership and control. This will accomplish several desirable goals. The procedure is simple, and it can be done alone or in small groups.

PROCEDURE

It is easy to say this is a simple procedure. This does not imply, however, that all your students will be proficient at this task initially. Many students have never questioned anything they've read, seen, or been told. No one expected them to. There was little in the way of invitation to do so. Yet they do ask random questions. As an experiment, you ought to try keeping tracking of all the questions you are asked by your students for a single day. Every time a student asks you a question, write it down. This is an effective metacognitive activity for you because it will make you far more deeply aware of what your students think are appropriate things to ask about at school, or at least in your classroom. If you are typical, the questions you will find yourself recording are mainly procedural questions. Procedural questions are questions that seek clarification or permission about whether, how, when, what, and so on, something is to be done or will occur. These are not questions that probe content or values. Here are some examples:

- ◆ "Did you say to do all the problems on page 36?"

- ◆ "Is this going to be on the test?"

- ◆ "Can I go to the bathroom?"

- ◆ "Joey's bothering me, can I move?"

- ◆ "What are we having for lunch?"

- ◆ "Can I get a drink of water?"

- ◆ "I don't understand how to invert the divisor."

- ◆ "Can we do something for extra credit?"

These are practical, important questions, important at least to the questioner. However, they are not questions that search deeply or probingly into meaning, purpose, truth, desire, hope, or morality. Young children, preschoolers and primary-level students, do ask probing questions. They want to know why the sky is blue, why dogs can't talk, why you have to sleep at night, what happens to someone when they die. They tend to be little scientists and philosophers, dedicated to finding out how things work, and why things are the way they are. This is their way of organizing and adapting to their world. Seemingly though, the longer students stay in school, the less they tend to ask profound questions. This is especially true of graduate students!

There is nothing wrong with procedural questions, per se. One is better off than not to know when an assignment is due, how many pages are required, and so on. But intellectually and morally a school environment ought to demand more of its teachers and students. A thoughtful school environment ought to encourage questions of substance, questions that require reflection, that seek understanding, that promote a sense of wonder, and that support curiosity and risk taking.

Another take on the question authoring activity is to introduce a lesson to the class, tell them the topic and perhaps, offer a brief preview of what is at stake. At this point, which is perhaps no more than five minutes into the lesson, you stop and ask each student to write down as many questions as they can think of that interests them about the topic. Students are then placed in dyads (pairs) and asked to compare the questions they have composed. As students volunteer their questions, you write them on the board and incorporate them into the lesson. It is one way to involve students in planning instruction.

OUTCOMES

I said earlier that *question authoring* by students achieves several educational outcomes. Among those outcomes are comprehension of subject matter, improved questioning skills, and reflective thinking about moral, practical, and intellectual purpose. Let's look at each in turn.

Question authoring serves as an aid to comprehension because it affords the learner an added perspective or an additional reason for reading, viewing, listening, participating, and so on. Let us say, for example, that a group of middle school students has been assigned Washington Irving's short story, *Rip Van Winkle*. At one level, we expect them to read the story and be able to discuss or answer questions about it. But if we ask our students to read the story *and* pose several questions about what they read, then they play a dual role during the process. Let us imagine that a student writes the following question: "How long did Rip Van Winkle sleep in the mountains?" The question is merely one of recall, the answer, 20 years, can be looked up and verified. Still, it is an important fact in the story, and therefore worth knowing. If this same student were required to write five questions about the story, comprehension is improved even if all the questions are merely recall level. But there is far more to the art of questioning. In time you will want your students to pose questions of explanation, application, analysis, and judgement.

Remember, we get good at what we practice. And when good coaching (teaching) accompanies our practice, we get even better. Therefore, if you consistently ask your students to write questions about what they are learning, they will get better at it. Their comprehension will improve, and their interrogatory skills will improve. You will see more and more higher level questions from them over time. This is an opportunity to teach them about *Bloom's Taxonomy* or some other version of a hierarchy of question-asking skills.

Once your students have a grasp of the idea that questions can range from hose that seek recall and comprehension of information to those that seek analysis, synthesis, and judgement, they can search for an appropriate balance in their question posing. Improvement will come with practice. I guarantee you that in time you will come to depend on your students as a source of good questions to use in discussions, activities, and assessment. And your students will come to think of themselves as individuals capable of asking questions that will take them to the heart of the matter, whatever the subject.

Consider the following problem-solving activity. What question could you write about it?

QUESTIONS DEVELOPED BY STUDENTS
FOR PROBLEM-SOLVING ACTIVITY

♦ All dice are alike in their configuration of spots. Spots on opposite sides add up to 7.

♦ What number is on the bottom of die A?

♦ What number of spots must appear on the blank face of die B?

♦ Three sides of die C do not carry the 2, 3, or 6 spots. What are the spots? Put them in proper places.

POST IT UP

> Posters of the sea and land, Thus do go about, about.
> William Shakespeare

PURPOSE

In Colonial America there were people known as pamphleteers who regularly attempted to get their ideas across to the public by posting notices. Perhaps the most famous of these was Thomas Paine, a leader of the American independence movement. His pamphlet, *Common Sense,* served to stir the heart of many a Colonist. Martin Luther used a similar technique in 1517 when he posted his *95 Theses* on the door of the church in Wittenburg. At a less dramatic level, just walk through a neighborhood in spring and count the posted notices of yard sales, meetings, and so on. The posting of notices is a time-honored means of communication. We truly need outlets for civil, public communication in classrooms. Discussions are useful, to be sure, but alternative means are also necessary.

The *Post It Up*[*] strategy is designed to afford students and teachers opportunities to make their ideas, insights, suggestions, and notes of encouragement public. The idea is that the commentary should be brief enough to write on a "post it" note, the kind of small square pieces of colored paper that have a strip of adhesive along the backside. When such notepaper is not available, the idea will still work using small cards or pieces of paper, which can be taped up around the room.

PROCEDURE

The *Post It Up* technique is a way to communicate without necessarily talking or directly engaging others. Thus, if a student has an idea or suggestion to make, he or she can write it down on the note and place it in some reasonable spot in the room. If the message is simply one of encouragement from one student to another, then the note can be placed on the recipient's desktop. It is actually a low-tech version of e-mail!

A primary use of *Post It Up* is as a kind of ubiquitous suggestion box. When students are working on projects or doing problem solving, thoughts will occur to them of a nature that does not demand the interrupting of the group or others

---

[*]   I am indebted to N.J. Petersen, who suggested the idea for this strategy.

at the time. There will be time enough later to take up the suggestion. By having a place to store and post ideas, we ensure that they will not be lost.

It is a common thing for students to be disciplined for passing notes during class time. But a reasonable question is, "Why do they do it?" The answer is typically that they wish to communicate something to someone else without necessarily drawing everyone else's attention to that fact. This is a problem waiting to be turned into a solution. Why not encourage students to communicate this way? If you have created the kind of classroom environment that supports student-to-student communication, builds trust, and encourages connections, then you need not be overly worried that their attempts to communicate with each other will be primarily devious, off task, and destructive of learning.

OUTCOMES

Post It Up is particularly useful if you are attempting to create an atmosphere of civility, respect, and mutual support. A note of encouragement from a teacher or a fellow student goes a long way toward making people feel welcome, involved, and encouraged. *Post It Up* gives students an ongoing opportunity to take the initiative in this regard.

Can it be overdone? I suppose it could be. Personally, I'd rather err on the side of too many ideas, notes of encouragement, and supportive statements than not. Can it turn into a negative thing? Yes, it could. But whatever it turns out to be will reflect the underlying social and moral conditions that have been cultivated in the classroom. Therefore, I am assuming that this will not be something to give you undue concern. And if a certain number of the notes are negative in tone, then you have a *real*, not a contrived issue to discuss with your class, itself an opportunity for problem solving and reflective thought.

KEY IDEA
IDENTIFICATION

> *An invasion of armies can be resisted, but*
> *not an idea whose time has come.*
> Victor Hugo

PURPOSE

The philosopher Alfred North Whitehead wrote that, "the first thing to do with an idea is to prove it." He went on to say that what he meant by "prove" an idea is to "prove its worth." Whitehead takes his place among many great educational thinkers who are convinced that trying to cover too many things is intellectually unproductive. His advice to teachers was, "do not teach too many subjects, …and what you teach, teach thoroughly," Essentially, he is saying that key ideas have staying power and that they should be carefully chosen and carefully emphasized by teachers. He points us gently toward the *quality* of the experience, not the quantity of material covered.

One way to think about the educational power of ideas is to consider what you'd like to have your students remember about a particular subject a year from now or into the future. You can test how well this worked for you. Recall your own second grade year, sixth grade, eleventh grade. What things do you remember from a particular class? If the teacher was successful with the subject matter and the experience in general, you will remember two things: the *feelings* and the *ideas*. The feelings should be positive, and the ideas should be few, but powerful.

PROCEDURE

As an assessment strategy, *Key Idea Identification* asks students to thoughtfully consider a lesson or series of related activities and to specify what they think is the key idea, main theme, or concept. Here is how it works.

At the close of a lesson or activity, ask students to identify what they think was the main or key idea. Of course, it helps to hold discussions from time to time on such topics as "What is an idea?" "Are ideas and skills different, and if so, how?" "When you read a book or listen to a presentation, how can you tell ideas from information?" Don't be surprised if your students have never discussed such questions.

When you ask students to identify the key idea of a lesson, give them a little room to make interpretations. Their idea of the idea may differ from yours. A good reflective session can happen after you have collected 25 or 30 impressions and compared and contrasted them with your own sense of the key idea.

A variation on the *Key Idea* theme is to have students, in small groups of three, discuss their own perspectives on the key idea of a lesson just completed. This provides them with the opportunity to think aloud as they reflect on the lesson and separate the wheat from the chaff. In addition to identifying the key idea, students should be asked to explain *why* this is the key idea. It represents a review, but more than that. It is a review in search of essence. The quest is to figure out what is at the heart of the matter.

OUTCOMES

Several significant outcomes should occur from the search for key ideas. One of the outcomes is aimed directly at the teacher. If you are going to have students identify the key idea of a lesson, then it makes sense for you to have one in mind before you teach the lesson. Thus you can raise your own level of consciousness about what you are doing. The researcher John Goodlad noted in his book, *A Place Called School,* that he seldom encountered classroom situations where teachers were teaching ideas. Mainly, he said, they teach information and skills. Goodlad concluded that either teachers do not think ideas are important or possibly they themselves do not think in terms of ideas. Neither thought is particularly encouraging, and you and I need to do something about it.

If students are to be asked to consider the key idea of an activity or lesson, or even of the week as a whole, then they too will need to raise their level of consciousness. They will have to think of learning as being composed of ideas. This is a good place to begin the processes of critical thinking, to consider how information can be put together to form knowledge, and how knowledge can serve as the foundation for ideas. This is the beginning of insight, that in time could lead to wisdom.

And finally, if teachers and students are looking for key ideas, then we have a clear signal that ideas are valued. This means that students need to think about the key idea(s) they wish to communicate in their writing, conversation, drawing, constructing, and other forms of expression. Thus teaching, learning, and reflective assessment come together to form a harmonious whole.

Try the following activity, "The Walking Path Simulation," with a class of students. After the students have played the game, ask them to identify the key idea.

THE WALKING PATH SIMULATION

Rules and Procedure:

1. A Walking Path will be built from the southern part of town to the northern part.

2. The problem is that several obstacles lie along the way. They include hills, swamps, streets, and houses.

3. City engineers are reluctant to build the path over hills because to do so raises construction costs. The Wildlife League does not want the path built through or near swamps because it could endanger fragile habitats. The Safety Commission does not want the path built across or near streets. The Housing Commission does not want the path built through people's homes and yards.

4. Each student is assigned one of the four roles listed above. City Engineer; Wildlife League; Safety Commission, Housing Commission.

5. The object of the simulation is for each player to draw a path starting from any of the squares on the southernmost half and ending with one of the squares on the northernmost half of the game board. For each square a player's path goes through, he or she must add five points to the total. In addition, players are penalized five points per square when they enter any square that causes problems from their particular perspective. Thus an Engineer must add five points to any square he or she enters that has a hill in it; Wildlife people must add five points to squares they enter that have a lake or swamp; Safety people must add five points to any square with streets; and Housing people five points to any square with houses. It is important to understand that the penalty is assessed to entry into any square with one of these impediments whether the path actually touches the impediment or not.

6. After each player has individually planned a path, students gather together in groups of four (one if each role) and plan a jointly agreed-to path. A total score is derived by adding up each player's individual score for the agreed-on plan. The challenge is to please each player, as much as possible while keeping in mind that compromise is always necessary in a democracy where different interests are at stake.

East

North

South

West

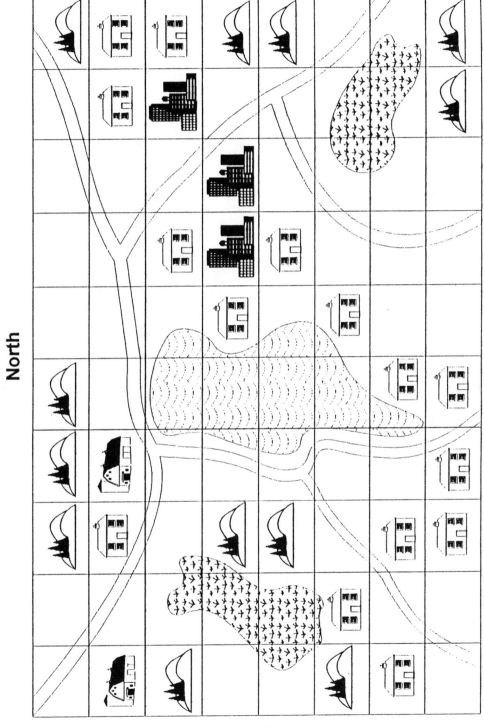

SEARCH FOR MEANING

> *Learning, in the proper sense, is not learning
> things, but the meaning of things.*
> John Dewey, *How We Think*

PURPOSE

A crucial difference in whether you or I learn something is the meaning or lack of meaning we attach to it. Meaning isn't the only variable in learning, but it is a powerful one. If something is meaningful, we respond, become animated and involved. Think of yourself playing in an important game, or short of that, being part of the crowd shouting yourself hoarse for the home team. Maintaining your attention is hardly a problem. If something seems less than meaningful, we find ourselves drifting off, becoming bored or uninterested. Have you ever walked by a classroom where students obviously were finding little meaning in whatever was going on? Typically, in their boredom, they will glance pathetically at you as though they are trying to make contact with humanity.

A young person learning to drive a car, typically wants to learn because the activity has meaning. The same person who forgot to do his or her homework probably did so because it had low priority on some internal "meaningfulness" scale. Why do young people join gangs? Why do young people try out for athletic teams? Why do they participate in the school play? The choir? How can a teacher guide his or her students toward meaningful educational experiences?

Meaning, when applied to school experience, especially academic experience, is an elusive quality. The *search for meaning* in classroom experience represents one of the highest, most purposeful and most difficult quests for teachers and students. Few pursuits have greater metacognitive potential. Like most reflective strategies, the *search for meaning* must begin with oneself. Let's say you're teaching reading, mathematics, or music. What meaning does the subject matter have to you? Is it merely required? Is it something you mastered long ago and now are bored with? Just a job to do, or do you truly feel that what you are teaching is vitally needed by your students? You can't wait to share it with them? You feel that your own learning is extended through your teaching? No school subject has meaning apart from our desire to teach and learn it. It is the human connection that makes the difference. This is exactly why we need *you* in the classroom and not someone who sees teaching as just another job.

PROCEDURE

The *Search for Meaning* assessment strategy represents an attempt to reflect on the moral implications of the learning experience. Whether you and your students conduct this procedure as a written task for each individual, use a discussion group approach, or a combination of both, the questions include the following:

◆ In what ways does this activity (assignment, and so on.) have or not have meaning for me personally?

◆ How specifically might others benefit (or not) from the experience?

◆ Does this activity make my classmates and me better for having done it? In what ways?

◆ Is this a useful, practical experience? If so, how?

◆ Is this experience enjoyable and fulfilling in other ways?

◆ Is this a reasonable learning experience?

◆ Does this experience make me want to pursue this subject further?

◆ Is this experience truthful? Does it build up my (our) integrity?

◆ Are all of us, not just some of us, involved?

These questions represent a place to start the process of reflection and the search for meaning. I encourage you and your students to add others that address the specific issues and goals you are trying to achieve. To the extent that you and your students are willing to write about and discuss meaning in learning, a classroom becomes a more truthful, open, and humane place.

OUTCOMES

Don't expect too much from your students at the outset. They probably have seldom been asked to think, write, and talk about such questions. This is a time for patience on your part. It may not even have occurred to them that they should be raising issues of morality, importance, and meaning about their schoolwork. Improvement will come with time. As your students begin to realize that your own search for meaning in learning is genuine and that you deeply desire that for them, they will respond.

Two additional outcomes of the *Search for Meaning* strategy are worth mentioning. First of all, this is a practical strategy. It is eminently practical to know to what extent you and your students find the work you do to be useful and meaningful. Why would you *not* want to know that? Places of voluntary association know about such practical matters on the basis of whether people show up, and whether they encourage their friends to get involved. But school is compulsory, and therefore we must look for more subtle practical manifestations. This is the place of conversation, of writing, and other means of signaling level of commitment.

The second outcome is one of efficacy or empowerment. We tend to appreciate it when people genuinely want to know how we feel, what we think, and how meaningful we find something. It represents an invitation. It gives us a voice in matters. It implies that needed changes will be made. Such empowerment brings with it a sense of responsibility. Genuineness is a two-way street. Just as the invitation to speak up, to lead, to offer suggestions, is sincere, so must the responsibility to share one's best thoughts and ideas be sincere. We talk a great deal about leadership skills, here is an opportunity for students to develop them.

RECORD-KEEPING

> Let's look at the record.
>
> Presidential candidate Al Smith

PURPOSE

Several years ago, an intriguing finding was reported from studies at one of the nation's leading medical schools of patients suffering from hypertension (high blood pressure). The obvious treatments, alone and in combination, were tried in order to determine the best courses of action for treating this dangerous illness. The treatments included medications, diet, exercise, meditation, relaxation response, and a range of other interventions including placebos. Patients receiving treatment were routinely asked to monitor their blood pressure, taking it several times a day and recording the results on a chart.

Completely apart from their findings of the effects of the various treatments, doctors began to notice a lowering in patients' blood pressure that seemed to be associated with the record keeping itself. That is, a *correlation* was noted between keeping a record of one's blood pressure over time and a subsequent reduction in one's blood pressure. Of course, such a relationship does not imply cause and effect. How could putting numbers on a sheet of paper cause one's blood pressure to decrease? Isn't this a little like the old prediction that when soft drink sales increase so does the rate of death by drowning? The *cause* is neither; it is the warmth of the sun that causes people to drink more and swim more.

When it comes to reducing one's blood pressure, diet, exercise, and other interventions have indeed been shown to be *causative* agents. So where does record keeping come into the picture? The answer is simple: keeping a record increases one's level of awareness. It creates a deeper level of consciousness. And not keeping a record often leads to an exaggerated sense of reality.

People often underestimate the number of hours they watch television each day, but when they begin to keep a record of what and how much they watch, they typically begin watching less. Try this activity with your students. Have them estimate the number of hours they spend watching television and them have them actually keep a record for a week. It makes for a good discussion. Good records are the beginning of good assessment.

The person who takes the time to record his/her blood pressure several times a day is far less likely to eat that doughnut, far more likely to take a walk, far less likely to kick the dog in anger, simply because he/she is more aware of the problem itself. Similarly, the student who takes the time to record scores on daily assignments, quizzes, and tests, is more likely than not to think about the quality of his/her work. It represents a reality check, so that if we wish to improve, we have established a baseline against which to measure subsequent improvement.

PROCEDURE

There is nothing magic about record keeping. It's just a wise procedure. It tends to reduce the gap between how one imagines one is doing and how well one is doing, in fact. A report card grade ought not to be a big surprise. A student ought to know pretty much how he/she is doing in mathematics, social studies, spelling, or any other subject. Keeping the record tends to put teacher and student on the same page, so to speak. And students should be required to show their parents the records they keep at least once or twice during a reporting period. This way help can be given when it is really needed and not after the fact.

Records are routinely kept in sports and we should learn from the example. Everyone knows whether the team has a chance to go to the playoffs because everyone who is interested knows the team's record. Each player knows not only how the team is doing in the standings, but also, how he/she is doing as an individual.

I suggest that you require students to record their grades or marks on all papers, complete with topic, date, any comments, and the grade itself. As the entries reach a significant number, then they should be converted to graphs, charts, essays, or other means of showing trends. This is the raw material for discussions that students need to hold with their parents from time to time about their progress.

Of course, spelling scores, mathematics scores, and other more easily quantified items are obvious material for record keeping. A more subtle form is the idea of writing down each day a *sense* of one's progress in less quantifiable areas of the curriculum. While this is more "subjective," it does indeed give both student and teacher insight into the student's perceptions. As you have students do this, remind them to incorporate any kind of evidence that they can of their progress.

OUTCOMES

Requiring students to keep records of their achievement gives them the opportunity to work with *real* data (their own). When they compute averages, make graphs and charts, calculate where they stand in relation to a grade in a class, and write brief notes on their progress, they are *doing* the kinds of activities that we want them to learn in mathematics, science, English, social studies, and other subjects. Thus a level of transfer of learning is achieved, something that rarely happens in school life if we can believe the critics. The English philosopher Francis Bacon wrote that real inquiry always begins with facts, one's own facts. The inferences should follow the facts.

The keeping of records is also the beginning of history. In the same way that we know so much about life in ancient Egypt because the Egyptians were such careful record keepers, so too did the Egyptians themselves know a great deal about their lives, far more than did those other societies in which records were poorly kept. I once read of a tribe where all evidence of a person's existence, all his/her belongings, and so on, was destroyed when the person died. The person was never mentioned again by those who knew him or her. Thus the tribe had no story because the past did not exist. There simply was no record and therefore no history.

A student who acquires and applies the record keeping skill early on is given a method of organization that will prove useful across a range of life activities. Keeping a record of school achievement is the beginning of the student's work as a historian and as a person of greater awareness and deeper consciousness.

And finally, record keeping places the responsibility for how one is doing, where it belongs, with the individual. This is not to say that teachers should not keep their own records. Of course they must. But it is far better to have two sets of records than one. If a student keeps good records of his/her achievement, there is little reason for surprise grades to happen. Knowing how you are doing along the way is empowering. It gives you the opportunity to make changes where and when they are needed. Socrates' admonition, "know thyself," is helped toward fulfillment when we keep good records.

WRITE IT DOWN

> I never travel without my diary.
> Oscar Wilde

PURPOSE

The witty Irish comedian Hal Roach would often pause reflectively and dramatically following one of his better jokes, giving the audience ample time to roar with laughter. When the howling had finally subsided, he'd draw yet another laugh by saying, "Write it down." The idea was that, if you do you're sure to remember it, and you just might want to tell the joke to your friends.

One of the most meaningful advances in opportunities for reflective thinking and metacognition in recent years is the requirement by teachers that students keep a journal. Whole books have been written on this topic, many of them very useful. Journal keeping can serve a variety of purposes. I have included journal keeping as one of our strategies with respect to its function as a reflective assessment tool.

A journal or diary is one of the most important tools in the quest for a reflective life. I have friends who are enthusiastic journal keepers. They write in their journals every day. As a result, they visit important events at least four times: (1) the event itself; (2) the recording of the event; (3) the pleasure of reading about the event days, months, or years later; and (4) the clearer meaning and understanding of events in perspective. The difference in levels of awareness between the diarist and those who keep no written record of their lives is profound.

PROCEDURE

Following are seven key questions for you and your students to pose in order to improve the quality of the journal keeping experience:

1. How selective and strategic are my journal entries?

    To paraphrase the old Bob Seeger song, "what to leave in, what to leave out." To what extent do the entries reflect on the things we are studying? To what extent am I able to connect the school experience with my life experience in general? Unless connections are made, students will never achieve what the philosopher Alfred North Whitehead called "the seamless whole" in learning.

2. What ideas am I considering?

   We have noted elsewhere in this book that school is unfortunately seldom about ideas. Far more often it is about information, skills, and facts. The problem with such a focus is that such material is neither well noted at the time nor long remembered. Ideas, on the other hand, have staying power, they remain with us, not always the details but the essence. So there are two considerations here: (1) ideas must be a central part of the school experience, and (2) ideas should be explored in the journals students and teachers keep.

3. What are the sources of my thoughts and entries?

   It has been noted that the two main avenues of human growth and development are the ideas we encounter and the people we get close to. This is a good place to start, with ideas and relationships. Other things tend to fall into place in their wake. Students need to be encouraged to enter ideas from the books they read, the material they study, the discussions in which they are involved. Because keeping a journal represents writing as learning, it is useful to keep in mind Charles Osgood's observation that a person's writing is only as good as the books they read. But there is also an affective side to the matter, and this is the function of relationships with others. A good journal is a blend of thoughts *and* feelings.

4. What insights to personal growth am I gaining?

   The important terms here are *insights* and *personal*. Am I becoming more reflective? How? In what ways? Am I improving my character, becoming a better person? Am I more interested in learning? Do I seek knowledge beyond the minimal school requirements? Am I in closer touch with my feelings? Am I growing in the area of becoming more involved with others? To what extent am I reaching out to others?

5. To what extent is my technical writing improving?

   Much emphasis is placed on creative writing, and that is all to the good. However, most of us will spend far more time in life doing technical writing. Journals are a good place to focus this process because the writing tends to be far more genuine than that found in the typical grammar exercise. Thus issues of syntax, spelling, punctuation, and paragraph development, for example, can be taught at more teachable moments because the writing is real. One line of argument is that students' journals should not be marked up with red pencil to the point that they are afraid to express themselves for fear of correction. I tend to agree. It is more useful to look for common errors in student writing and to construct teaching episodes that address those errors generally. Where specific help is needed, that can be made a matter of individualized instruction.

6. How honest am I?

A climate of trust is essential. Students need to know that you will always respect their confidences and that they can and should take risks with their thoughts and feelings. Anything short of this fails to meet the goal of a reflective, metacognitive learning environment. As students come to know that you will respect their work, you should expect greater honesty of expression.

7. What provisions are made for feedback?

We have already addressed the matters of grammatical and technical issues in journal writing. Now we can address the larger picture. Your feedback should be based on the premise that you have actually read the journals, and beyond that, your remarks should reflect the first four questions posed in journal keeping. You need to constructively criticize and support your students' efforts to explore ideas, to go to the best available sources, to include appropriate content, and to show some measure of insight in their writing.

OUTCOMES

Keeping a journal expands the thought processes and provides a means of personal exploration and reflection. Its very privacy, intimacy, and personal content make it a powerful avenue for learning. Because each individual decides what he/she will enter in the journal, the experience is customized, allowing for and inviting different perspectives, different senses of what really matters, and a unique opportunity for each person to express those things that have the greatest individual relevance and meaning. So, *Write It Down!*

ALL THINGS CONSIDERED

Personal perspective…is the only kind of history that exists.
Joyce Carol Oates

PURPOSE

The failure to connect ideas represents one of the most fundamental problems in teaching and learning. When ideas are not considered reflectively and connected they remain inert, that is, they start nowhere and go nowhere intellectually. Instead, they are deposited in the short-term memory bank, a place where they draw very little interest. The best hope seems to be able to remember them for the test, a poor investment that yields a poor rate of return indeed.

The *All Things Considered* strategy asks students and teachers to take a few minutes at the end of the day, when the time comes in the afternoon that the day is a history that began that morning, to think back over the things that happened, and to see whether some of them might in some ways be related or connected, and if so, how they might be connected. This search for connections should cause students to focus on the *essence* of the activities and lessons in which they were engaged. It should bring about some sort of inquiry into what the day at school was "all about."

PROCEDURE

Let me give you an example. In a science class students had been studying the five simple machines: lever, screw, wheel and axle, pulley, and wedge. One of the principles the class had been taught, and was supposed to have learned, is that machines increase our ability to accomplish tasks by making our efforts more efficient. A person can use a lever, for example, to lift a heavy object by pushing down (and therefore taking advantage of gravity) rather than by lifting up. Thus a key idea or concept is *efficiency*. There are other ideas, of course, including force, gravity, and distance, to name a few.

To identify an important concept from a school subject and to apply it to other learning experiences is a rather simple and straightforward idea, but how often does it happen at school? The answer is, not often. Why is this? It seems that the barriers built up between and among school subjects are nearly insurmountable. Sometimes this is so because teachers teaching the various subjects fail to communicate with one another about what they are teaching making it difficult to make connections from one class to another. In other cases, a teacher may be teaching all the subjects, but the textbooks he/she uses are not correlated in any meaningful ways, so even the teacher fails to make connections. But this is not as it should be. Any subject worth our serious attention will have touch points with other spheres of learning. The secret is to go after those touch points, identify them, and think through the connections.

To return to our example from science class, let's go in search of connections to the concept of efficiency. One student mentions that in social studies the class learned about the method used by the Arawak Indians of the Caribbean to plant corn, beans, and squash together in mounds instead of rows so that the roots would intertwine, giving the plants strength against hurricane winds and tropical rains. This was a model of efficiency as the Spanish learned the hard way when they forced the Indians to use the European method of planting in rows and the hurricanes blew the crops away. This is the idea, to see that a concept has more than one application.

The teacher asks whether anyone can give another example of efficiency, either from other classes or from any area of life. Someone else points out that a grocery shopping list is an example of efficiency because it keeps you from forgetting certain things you need and because it should keep you from buying things you don't need. Another student mentions that keeping a record of your own progress is efficient because it keeps you informed and serves as a reminder of how you're doing. Yet another student notes that, when you're beginning to do research on a topic, it is efficient to do an on-line search of possible information sources and to create a file of key sources.

On the basis of this discussion, a reflective thinking assignment emerges, one that illustrates the point that a teacher need not fear that making interdisciplinary connections will "water down" a given subject. The assignment is for each student to do two things: (1) interview an adult about efficiency in his/her own work; and (2) identify a simple machine in the real world, draw it, make a model if possible, and explain how it works.

The first task expands the concept beyond the science subject matter, and the second task brings the concept right back to the subject matter itself, raising the level of understanding to real world applications. Thus, if a student interviews a coach and learns that one way the coach practices efficiency is to have a routine established for practice sessions, this represents an expansion of the concept. And if a student studies a can opener or an automobile jack, then the focus is back onto simple machines and their application.

OUTCOMES

An abiding purpose of assessment is to enable the teacher to reflect on his/her own practice. By encouraging students to make connections between and among subjects, a teacher has gone a long way toward creating a more coherent curriculum and a curriculum that has important ideas at its center. So when all things are considered, the level of consciousness of both students and teachers is raised.

For the elementary teacher, it helps to have a list of key ideas posted and to encourage students to connect those ideas as the day moves along from reading to mathematics, to social studies, to science, to art, and to music. At secondary levels, especially where subjects are taught independently of one another and where students in any given class will not have attended other classes together, the very least a faculty can do is to create a list of key concepts that are emphasized and reemphasized across the curriculum.

The point of *All Things Considered* is to help students make connections between and among subjects and activities. The more they are able to do this, the more the school day approaches coherence. And as they expand the connections to the world around them, they begin to see the strategic, applied importance of the things they are learning at school.

I CAN TEACH

> *Practical education includes skill, discretion, and morality.*
>
> Immanuel Kant

PURPOSE

Aristotle noted, some 25 centuries ago, that a sure way to learn something is to be given the opportunity to teach it. He was right then and he is right now. Teachers, especially college professors who teach the same subject term after term, year after year know this little secret. It starts to sink in. Teaching as learning works particularly well when the teacher is also an enthusiastic learner.

Teaching functions best when a symbiotic relationship develops between the desire to learn new knowledge and skills and the corresponding desire to share what one has learned and continues to learn with others. Invariably, the best teachers are those who are eager to learn their subject matter and who want more than anything to share their enthusiasm for learning with the young. When knowing, sharing, and caring come together, people will learn. You can't hold them back.

PROCEDURE

The *I Can Teach* strategy puts the student into the dual role of learner and teacher. It challenges him or her to learn something not merely to acquire knowledge or to pass a test, but to learn something well enough to be helpful to others. There is a deeply imbedded, empowering moral purpose here, and that is that knowledge, good knowledge, knowledge worth gaining, is also worth sharing with others.

The payback is wonderful. The learner who becomes a teacher will take his or her own understanding to deeper levels while experiencing the joy of seeing someone else begin to understand. This is basically the model that was used in Mexico some years ago to increase literacy throughout the country. The project there was called "each one teach one." The idea was that each person who was taught to read was asked to teach someone else to read in turn. It was enormously successful, and the literacy rate soared.

Here is how the *I Can Teach* strategy proceeds. At the conclusion of a lesson or series of lessons around a common theme, you challenge your students to think about and write down, diagram, or map a way that they could *teach* what they just *learned* to someone else. This is obviously effective with "older" students who teach something to "younger" students, for example, fifth graders teaching an idea to first graders. Of course, the technique can also be applied at peer levels or by having students teach something they learned to their parents. Let us look at each of these three applications in more detail.

Students who are challenged to teach something they have learned to younger learners must take several things into account. First of all comes the abiding question, "How well do I know this skill, idea, or content?" The answer must be something like, "I know this at a deeper level than just that of memory or passing exam questions that demand only recognition or recall."

If, for example, the challenge is for secondary students to teach elementary students the Pythagorean Theorem ($a^2 + b^2 = c^2$), then the secondary students who will teach this must have learned more deeply than merely memorizing the formula. The psychologist Jerome Bruner wrote many years ago that it is possible to teach anything to anyone if it is done in an intellectually honest way. If this is so, what kinds of accommodations would be necessary in order for, say, fourth graders to learn this mathematical idea? Obviously, the "teacher" would need to use concrete materials or something oriented towards a "hands-on" approach. But the point is that fourth graders *are* capable of learning this.

The key is found in *how* someone is taught. I remember a conversation I had once with a person who had successfully completed several courses in advanced mathematics who told me that she never understood the Pythagorean Theorem in any concrete sense. But she did remember passing exams where "knowledge" of the theorem was required.

Applied at a peer level, the *I Can Teach* strategy is useful as a means of bringing certain students up to speed on an idea or skill. The coverage mentality so prevalent in our schools compels teachers to keep moving on to the next lesson in order to complete the curriculum. It is an unfortunate mentality and one that can hardly be endorsed by thoughtful people, but it is nevertheless a reality. Often when something is taught, a certain number of students seem to grasp the idea the first time. Many others either understand it imperfectly or not at all.

The effect of this over time is devastating. Students who are not quick to grasp what is taught fall hopelessly behind. The irony is that those who are quick to grasp something are not necessarily ultimately better at understanding, just quicker. In fact, some students who exhibit a kind of plodding, deliberate style are, in fact, capable of learning in profound ways. if given enough time. In spite of the wisdom of Aesop's fable of *The Tortoise and the Hare,* many teachers have yet to learn that swift is not always better than slow. So, *I Can Teach* affords a perfect opportunity for those who *do* understand an idea or skill to teach it to their classmates who do not. Everyone will benefit.

A third application of *I Can Teach* is as a homework assignment in which students are asked to teach something they have learned in your class to their parents or brothers and sisters. This serves several purposes.

♦ First, it is a communications tool between school and home. Parents get a chance to find out experientially what their child is being taught at school; awareness is created, linkages are formed.

♦ Second, the student is given another opportunity to revisit the material, this time from the perspective of explainer. This is reinforcement of something important at its best. One of your long-range goals ought to be to create conditions for parents and children to talk to each other. This gives them a reason to do so and a vehicle for doing it.

♦ Third, when students report back on the success of their venture at home, then the material is visited for yet a third time. What if students had trouble teaching the idea? This tells you something you need to hear. Remember, anything worth learning is worth learning well.

I recommend a procedure whereby you give students an opportunity to put on paper their ideas for teaching the activity. Of course, younger students will need to do this orally. Once students have written down or diagramed their ideas, they should form triads (groups of three) that meet for 15 minutes or so in order to share insights, ideas, methods, materials, or whatever else might be needed to teach the content effectively. To the extent that you think it is helpful, you can take an active part in making suggestions, especially the first few times you use this strategy.

It is crucial that you have follow-up discussions which focus on how well things went. This is a way of reflecting back on the experience in order to make sure that improvement occurs over time. By the time the year ends, you will have sown a whole new crop of teachers.

OUTCOMES

I Can Teach is designed to empower students with the thought that knowledge is something you use, not just something you keep in the storehouse of the mind until examination time. This strategy asks students to cross a threshold from learning as something only for oneself, to learning as something you pass along to others. Learning is transformed from acquisition to performance. You, yourself, know the pleasure of helping people learn. It is time to share that pleasure with your students. Use it or lose it.

**A STUDENT'S NOTES FOR TEACHING THE
PYTHAGOREAN THEOREM TO YOUNGER STUDENTS**

I will use blocks or squares from graph paper. I will ask my brother to measure. My little brother will make the diagram. I will ask him how he feels and what he learned.

Rebecca, 8th grade

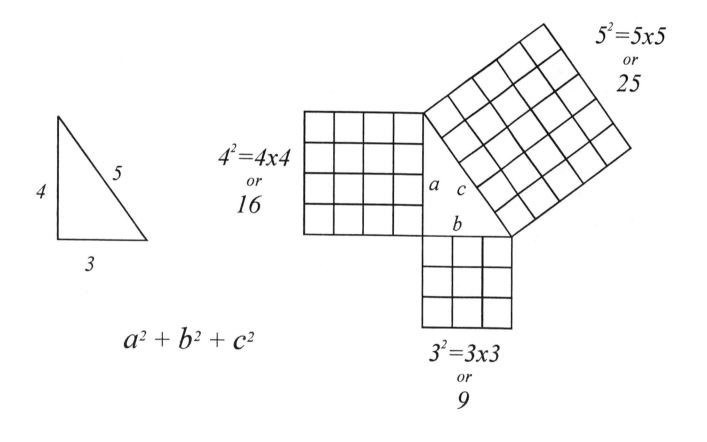

$$a^2 + b^2 + c^2$$

CIRCLE MEETING

The power of the world always works in circles.
Black Elk

PURPOSE

Several decades ago, Dr. William Glasser introduced an idea designed to give teachers and students a systematic way of voicing their concerns, thoughts, and attitudes. He called it the *Circle Meeting*. As the name implies, students and teacher sit in a large circle and are each given an opportunity to speak, in turn. When it is a given individual's turn to say something, he or she can voice an opinion, state a concern, raise an issue, or whatever comes to mind related to the meeting's purpose. It is also an option for the individual who chooses not to speak to say, "I pass." Going systematically around the circle gives everyone an opportunity to contribute while restraining the more talkative types from monopolizing the conversation.

The benefits of the *Circle Meeting* strategy are several. First of all, it is a public forum, that is, everyone who is part of the class is expected to attend. Therefore, any concerns or issues that are raised are heard by everyone at the same time. This is a real plus because it reduces the ambiguity about how someone may think or feel. No one is needed to "broker" the expression of a given individual. Also, people may, if they wish, take the opportunity to raise their hands to ask clarifying questions of the speaker. A second benefit is one I alluded to previously, that is, because of the structured response procedure, everyone has the same opportunity to be involved. One of the ongoing frustrations of whole class "discussions" is that many students never speak a word and a few students tend to do most of the talking. Thus, even if the sentiments expressed are useful and valid to a point, neither teacher nor the class really know how many students feel or think about things. This limits us from knowing the full truth of a situation, because the truth of a social situation can be discovered only through full disclosure.

A third point about the *circle meeting* is that it is practical. Things may or may not be going well in mathematics, science, English, or in class in general but, by circling up once a week or so, we can take our temperature so to speak. We can know what others think and how they see things. If things are going well, we want to know that. Where there may be trouble spots or problems it is good to catch them early on.

It is useful at this point to revisit the "trust" issue in teaching, learning, and assessment, together. The strategies found in this book will or will not work well for a variety of reasons, but one of the most foundational issues at stake is trust. Trust between you and each individual student is at stake every time you ask students to write down or express orally their ideas about what they're learning. Do they trust you enough to be completely honest with you? If so, expect considerable insight from your students. Expect them not only to assess their own learning, but expect them to be helpful to you as you reflect on the goodness, usefulness, and propriety of what you're trying to teach. If not, expect them to be guarded in their responses, always trying to say what they think you want them to say. This serves no one well.

There is also the issue of trust between and among all those who are part of the class. Do students feel free to speak their mind without fear of ridicule? Do they think that others genuinely care about what they have to say? Do they think that when they speak others might benefit from their insights? Do they look forward to hearing from their fellow classmates in order to get a better sense of perspective? Are there feelings of unity and *esprit de corps*? Do students support each other while feeling free to disagree on issues? Are friendships being made? These are the deeper, more abiding aspects of assessment that many teachers and their students never countenance.

PROCEDURE

Practical questions, such as how many times should we go around the circle, inevitably arise. My suggestion to you is that the first time you use this strategy, just go around once. Give each person one chance to contribute. It is good to take some notes as the students speak unless you feel that this will inhibit them. Later on when you have time, write down your thoughts about how the meeting went. In time, you may want to expand the opportunities, allowing several trips around the circle. You are probably the best judge of how productive it is to limit or expand the number of times around. A rule of thumb is that it is better to end an activity while it is going well than to prolong it to the point of boredom. In other words, stay in the flow.

Another practical question is, "How do we regulate the amount of talking by each student?" Keep in mind that the process is structured. This means that you go around the circle in order and each person gets to say one thing. This is pretty close to equal opportunity.

Ground rules are important. We are not here to criticize others, to say hurtful things, or to speak in inappropriate ways. The process is orderly, civil, and inclusive. It is useful for you to take notes in order to document the record unless you feel that your note taking has an inhibiting effect on the group.

OUTCOMES

As reflective practice, the *circle meeting* should provide you and your students with a time to examine thoughts, feelings, hopes, and concerns. It involves some risk taking by all involved. When it works, you have a more honest environment. There is little honesty in a so-called social environment when members of the group hardly know what others are thinking. You also will find yourself collecting a wide range of ideas from your students because you are inviting them to speak up, to share, and to show concern for how well things are going. Good ideas, like gold, are where you find them, and I guarantee they are there for the finding in your classroom. The *circle meeting*, when it works well, is a time and place of support and encouragement. You'll be pleased, for example, when the student who says that he/she is having trouble with the assignments, finds that several classmates are more than willing to help. Trust takes time and patience. Improvement comes with practice.

THANK YOU

> *Thank you for being a friend.*
> James Taylor

PURPOSE

Try to think of a time in your life when someone did something for you or taught you something for which you were truly grateful. Often, the kind of thing that comes to mind is something like an unexpected gift, favor, or perhaps the time you learned to ride a bicycle, drive a car, or learned to swim. These are dramatic, empowering events.

Much of school learning, of course, is incremental. We add a little bit more to what we already knew and the learning typically tends to blend with prior knowledge in something less than dramatic fashion. Occasionally there are exceptions. Psychologists and learning theorists tell us that we know half of what we will ever know by the time we are five years old, so it is true that much of our acquired knowledge came to us at an age when we took learning for granted and probably weren't aware enough of others to thank them. But we continue as life-long learners, and our teachers are many. And to the extent that this is true for you and me, we owe a debt of gratitude.

It is not unusual for us to read a book recommended to us by a friend. The friend and the book's author each taught us something. This is informal, just as a spirited conversation in which you and others exchange ideas may represent an informal learning situation. Typically, the more spirited the conversation, the less it has to do with school, but you are going to change that!

Many adults enroll in classes of one kind or another, not for the credit, but just to learn. It is estimated that adult Americans are so eager to learn, that the average person spends one to two hours per week in classes of one kind or another. So, we continue throughout our lives to seek out learning opportunities, many which are organized by caring teachers.

Our focus here is on the classroom, that is, the present time for students. But an educational goal to which we subscribe as teachers of the young is that of instilling lifelong learning habits. And to the extent that we are successful, our students will continue on a learning path long after the year or so that they typically spend with us. They will seek out teachers, and they themselves will teach others. It is to those who take the time and energy to teach us that the *Thank You* strategy is dedicated. It is well to keep in mind a definition of teaching as the creating of conditions, environments and opportunities to learn. Therefore, someone who recommends a good book or an idea is by this definition a teacher.

PROCEDURE

Like the other assessment strategies found in these pages, *Thank You* serves several reflective functions. For the author of a *thank you* note, there is the opportunity to think about something of significance that he/she has learned, and to express feelings of gratitude toward the person who played an instrumental role in the learning that occurred. The more specific the note, the more the writer is able to revisit what he/she has learned, thus allowing aspects of analysis, synthesis, and evaluation to come to the forefront. And because the *Thank You* strategy is an affective as well as a cognitive experience, the writer taps the deep well of emotions and feelings that inevitably attach themselves to true and meaningful learning.

There is also a reflective function for the recipient of the *thank you* note. In many cases, you will be the recipient. I guarantee it. As you receive these notes over time, you will notice that patterns emerge. You may find repeated expressions of gratitude for your kindness, patience, support, friendliness, understanding, concern, high expectations, and so on. You'll notice a moral fabric emerging, stitched together by your students, one that any teacher would aspire to. You'll also come to a far deeper understanding of what your students value in your teaching efforts.

Like anything else we do in life, we improve with practice. Young children will author simple *thank you* notes in words and pictures. Accept these sincere expressions of gratitude with a thankful heart. Your own *thank you* notes to students, colleagues, and parents will serve as models of specificity from which others will learn. Keep in mind that some of your students will find it difficult initially to express their thanks, even when they are thankful. Perhaps this is because they, themselves, have so seldom been thanked for anything they've done. This makes your role as model all the more significant.

OUTCOMES

The historian David Hamilton wrote that manners are close to morality. By this he meant that, when we show kindness, respect, and gratitude toward others, a more civil environment begins to take shape. You will begin to see a change toward a more polite and mannerly atmosphere in the classroom if your students begin to take for granted the idea of thanking others. You will also see a heightened level of interdependence. You'll find yourself writing *thank you* notes to students for specific acts of helping, trying, supporting, caring.

One final note of caution, *this procedure is both contagious and habit forming.* Your students will start thanking each other, the principal, counselor, music teacher, coach, custodian, cafeteria workers, neighbors, parents, and others in their lives. Things can get quickly out of control, and people you aren't directly responsible for teaching, people you don't even know in some cases, will be sending each other *thank you* notes because of what you have started. It's an old idea, one we've lost track of to a certain extent, and its effects are powerful.

PARENTS ON BOARD

Show kindness to parents.
The Qur'an

PURPOSE

It is widely known that parents are potentially the most important factor in a child's education. I say potentially, because while they do have the power to be of great influence, there are times that it seems that some of them at least are content to "let the schools take care of my child's learning." This is a mistake of tragic proportions. The philosopher Jurgen Habermas notes that one of the most debilitating problems of our time is the rise of "expert" cultures that take the place of home and neighborhood in handling tasks that home and neighborhood ought to handle. For teachers and administrators the best approach, of course, is for school to work together with the home. This is the single most effective way to support a child's learning.

The *Parents on Board* strategy does what its name suggests, gets parents directly involved in their child's school work. It works best when it is used systematically and methodically. It is not designed to be an occasional approach to parent/child cooperation. This is so because it is an integrative strategy, that is, it is designed to *integrate* school life with home life.

PROCEDURE

Here is how it works. Parents need to be asked in specific, concrete ways to offer their help. Generic pleas for them to be involved may reach a few, but most won't know what you want of them in this regard. One approach, suitable with younger children, is to use a form which parents sign and which the children bring to you.

There are three levels of parent help that we will discuss here. They range from minimally engaged to high levels of engagement. The first level is simply a *concrete suggestion* of something for them to do to facilitate their child's learning. It may be as simple as asking them to ensure that their child has a specific time and place to do homework. In this regard, the request is about the same as that made by the piano teacher who asks parents to be sure that the child practices playing the piano for a certain number of minutes per day. As simple as this idea is, it really does work. The establishment of routines for carrying out important tasks is a lesson to be learned early in life, and homework is a good place to start the process. As a professional, you may be surprised to learn that some parents have not thought of the idea of providing a specific place and time for their child to do his/her homework, but remember, they need your advice and counsel more than you might know, especially the parents whose involvement levels are the lowest.

A second level of *Parents on Board* is that of helping a child to carry out his/her homework assignments in ways that go beyond mere enforcement of time and place. For example, if you suggest that it is beneficial for parent and child to take a walk at least one evening a week, to watch and critique a television program together, to make plans to do a project of some kind (not necessarily related to school) around the house or apartment, then you have *created the opportunity* for parents and children to interact in meaningful ways. If one can believe the surveys that tell us that fathers, for example, spend less than five minutes per day interacting with their children, then you will have at the very least attempted to do something about that.

A third level of *Parents on Board* is that of inviting parents to take part in the curriculum itself. A common refrain from parents, when their children reach intermediate and middle school years, is that the mathematics is too difficult for them to understand, much less be of help with. This is a perfect opportunity to start Family Mathematics Night once or twice a month, or Arts Night, or Geography Night, or Science Night, or Literature Night. You get the idea. By offering stimulating, engaging, easy-to-follow instruction to parents and their children together, you bring about a level of integration in the family that you might not have thought possible.

Some schools have benefited greatly by having everyone (teachers, students, and staff) read the same book. It creates conversational opportunities that spill over from class to class. Why not take this brilliant idea one step further and invite parents on board? Who knows what will happen when you get the entire school community reading, talking, and writing together?

OUTCOMES

My experience in explaining this strategy to teacher groups tells me that not everyone thinks this approach will work for the reason that a certain number of parents do not care enough to become involved. I have a couple of answers to this opposition, both of which are based on my own experience. The first is that we live in a less than perfect world. Of course, not every parent is going to follow every suggestion you or I make. This should not surprise us. But you might be surprised by how many will respond to your sincere suggestions for their child's education. My second answer is that we simply cannot know to what extent parents will cooperate until we try to find out. And much of the high art of teaching is found in the trying! You and I can never guarantee an outcome for someone else, but we can guarantee that we will try our best to help others learn.

I have seen primary through secondary schools, that have filled gyms, libraries, and cafeterias to capacity with Family Night activities related to the curriculum. Invariably, the payoff is tremendous, ranging from good will to more focused parent participation. If you are serious about raising academic achievement and improving the social/moral fabric of school life, then you must get parents on board.

FOCUS GROUPS

With three people there is something bold in the air:
direct things get said....To be three is to be
in public, you feel safe.
Elizabeth Bowen

PURPOSE

The focus group has its roots in group dynamics and social interaction theory. Typically a focus group is a small group given a specific task such as reacting to a television program that group members have just watched, or to a speech or a debate. The job of the focus group is to provide the feedback needed to make corrections, improvements, and so on. Such groups are used extensively by candidates for office and by pollsters interested in political trend analysis, as well as for market research purposes by manufacturers and advertisers.

PROCEDURE

The *Focus Group* strategy as an assessment technique utilizes a similar approach. The idea is for you to select any particular event, activity, assignment, or other experience in which the class has been involved and seek specific lines of feedback from *focus groups*. For example, at the conclusion of a unit on insects a teacher assigned *focus groups* in her class the following questions:

- ♦ What are some important ideas that you think you learned?

- ♦ What was difficult about the experience?

- ♦ What things were most interesting to you?

- ♦ How could the experience have been improved?

- ♦ Several years from now, what do you think you will remember from this?

Each group in the preceding example was composed of three members. Three is a good group size for a task of this nature. It is large enough to accommodate a range of ideas and perspectives, but small enough to allow each member to participate actively. Research done years ago in small group interaction by the investigator R. F. Bales[*] showed that a typical division of talk in a triad, or

---

[*] Bales, R.F. (1957). Effects of size of problem-solving groups on the system of interaction. *Report to the Annual Meeting of the American Psychological Association.*

group of three, is 42%, 34%, and 24% by the three participants. This is a fairly equitable distribution of talk time for group members. You may want to share this information with your students as a means of heightening their awareness of the importance of listening, as well as talking, in a small group. When small groups get much larger, certain members tend to dominate the talk, while others withdraw from active participation.

A reasonable amount of time for a *focus group* to meet for discussion is 15 to 30 minutes, depending on the depth of analysis required, as well as, on the social skills and age of the participants. Students often find it difficult to participate in a small group discussion, primarily because they have not had much practice in doing so. Patience is necessary on your part. They will improve with practice and with coaching tips regarding behavior in such a setting. A common complaint I have heard from teachers regards the one or two students who disrupt their small group.

A simple but effective management technique is for you simply to remove anyone from a *focus group* who is disruptive. Tell the person that he/she can complete the assignment alone. There is no reason for scolding or harsh disciplinary methods unless the situation is quite unusual. Rather, this is merely a natural consequence of the person's behavior. Perhaps next time the student will choose to be part of a group.

Whether each *focus group* records its answers is a matter of judgment on your part. I favor keeping a written record if possible. This allows you the luxury of going over the comments at your convenience in order to self-assess how things are going. At any rate, when the group discussions have run their course, it is time for the whole class to join together to present and listen to reports from each *focus group*. The fact that each group has already discussed the questions makes for a much more disciplined, focused whole class discussion. This part of the process also brings into play the practical aspect of fuller understanding of feelings and perspectives by the whole class.

The example cited above from the unit on insects merely provides us with a specific instance of the *focus group*. Keep in mind that the questions posed provide the focus and discipline necessary to the success of the group. On the other hand, it is good to allow groups to add a question or two or to address an issue that is not found in the questions. You never know what gems may emerge if you also give students a certain amount of free reign in addition to the specified task.

OUTCOMES

The outcomes from the *focus group* strategy should include: (1) the opportunity for individual students to voice their ideas and feelings and to hear their fellow students voice theirs; (2) the opportunity to compare individual and small group perspectives with those of other individuals and groups; and (3) useful feedback to the teacher who sincerely desires to include students in the process of making improvements in the teaching/learning experience.

AUTHENTIC APPLICATIONS

It does not pay to tether one's thoughts to the post of use with too short a rope.
John Dewey

PURPOSE

Most schoolwork is academic, perhaps not in the sense that it is always so intellectually challenging, but academic in the sense that it is not put to use. This is unfortunate because it is in the application of knowledge, skills, and values that human beings find meaning. When ideas are not applied, they seem to start nowhere and go nowhere.

Imagine practicing for a play, one in which you are given a significant role, and then learning that the point of the whole experience was practice. There will be no production, no costumes, no make-up, no opening night, no combination of fear, excitement, and anticipation, no audience, no reviews, no parties held after the performance. Just practice.

Or, imagine a basketball team that practices daily: free throws, passing, rebounding, jump shots from the corner, defense, and so on. Imagine also that the coach tells you and your teammates from the start that there will be no games, no crowd, no enthusiasm, no fans screaming themselves hoarse, no league, no popcorn sold, just good old fashioned practice. The whole idea seems preposterous. Why would we even consider it? The answer is that we would not.

Now let us focus on the classroom. Classrooms are places where great ideas are often introduced, ideas that have changed the world. This happens all the time in mathematics, history, art, literature, geography, science, and other curricular areas. If this is so, then why is typical schoolwork not more exciting and engaging? One answer to this question is failure to apply ideas. The key is not so much the idea itself, many lessons and activities contain ideas that have unlimited potential. But potential is just that, something that could occur but has not yet occurred, as in potential energy before it is transformed into kinetic energy.

The purpose of the *Authentic Applications* strategy is to challenge you and your students to become involved in ways that transform the curriculum from one of potential energy to one of applied, functioning energy. And the key to doing this is to find as many outlets for student work as possible.

PROCEDURE

Some of these outlets are obvious, just waiting for action. For example, when students do artwork such as painting, drawing, and sculpting, the usual routine is for their efforts to be sent home where some of it ends up decorating refrigerator doors. That is all right, but what about an intermediate step where the artwork done by the class is displayed at a senior citizens' home for a few days? This gives students an audience to think about and to share with, and it gives some retired folks a glimpse of school life. Who knows, perhaps some friendships will occur as a result.

Students in history classes often put together displays of state and local history, including maps, documents, sketches, essays, models, photographs, and oral histories. This is a perfect opportunity to contact the people at City Hall or some other government building to see whether they would like to have the work put on display there. The chances are good that they will accept.

The philosopher and academic leader Robert Maynard Hutchins, who served for many years as the Chancellor of the University of Chicago, an elite academic school, once remarked that the reason students like the extra curriculum so much is because the curriculum is so stupid. Hutchins noted the excitement, pleasure, rewards, and genuine learning that accompany the experience of being in the band or orchestra, the debate team, athletic teams, yearbook, school newspaper, or clubs. He contrasted this with the sterile, unappealing atmosphere of most classroom academic environments. It doesn't have to be that way, but it will take *you* to change things.

Two words come to mind to describe the extra curriculum: authentic and application. If you've ever worked on a school newspaper, you know that the authenticity derives from the fact that the newspaper is actually distributed and read by people. The deadlines are real, the grammar is applied, and the written word finds an audience.

Of course, not every lesson can be immediately applied. But the starting point is to decide right now that a great deal more of schoolwork *can* be authentically applied. This is why the best schools have science fairs, art fairs, concerts, games, something going all the time. These applications are the single best way to bring the public to the school and the school to the public. There is no better form of public relations for a school. And the key to all of this is to think in terms of projects. There should never be a time in your class when project learning is not emphasized. Projects are, by definition, authentic in that they are chosen by students, usually take team work, employ knowledge and skills as tools to be used, and result in some kind of display, performance, or other public outlet.

OUTCOMES

The reflective potential of *authentic applications* is great. When students have displayed their work, been involved in a performance or competition, applied their abilities to an actual outcome, then there is indeed something to talk about, critique, analyze, and take pleasure in. Mark Twain once noted that, in writing, the difference between choosing the right word and the wrong word to express a thought is as great as the difference between lightning and a lightning bug. I wish to submit for your consideration the idea that the difference between schoolwork that is mainly practice and schoolwork that is applied in some authentic way is just as great. When authentic applications are made, then effort, pride in one's work, and even the critique itself, take on a depth of meaning seldom found in typical schoolwork. "Practice sessions" even take on added significance, just as they do for an orchestra, the cast of a play, or an athletic team.

The theme of this book is teaching, learning, and assessment together to create reflective practice. Authentic applications of schoolwork help to create the necessary conditions. Knowing that your work will be displayed in some way changes the stage of preparation, so crucial in problem solving and creative effort. This foreknowledge enables a learner to think ahead to the event, lending a focus to the work. The stage in which the event itself takes place (science fair, athletic contest, play, or concert) offers further opportunity for reflection, judgment, review, and analysis. And stage three, when the performance is over, represents a time to reflect, to think about meaning, truthfulness, beauty, and effort, and to take the measure of what went right or wrong toward improvement in the future.

GET A JOB

> *What is work? And what is not work?*
> *Are questions that perplex the wisest?*
> Bhagavadgita

PURPOSE

There was a popular song in the late 1950s, sung by a group called The Silhouettes, the title of which was "Get a Job." The song told the story of a poor luckless fellow who tried, to find a job, all to no avail. Each night he read the papers, scanning the want ads and looking for work. But in a serious sense, getting a job is one of the outcomes that most students and parents hope for as a result of the school experience. We can talk about learning as an end in itself, and it is, but practical, pragmatic Americans want school to equip students with the skills and knowledge necessary to find a job and compete in the work place.

The *Get a Job* strategy represents an attempt to link school work with the world of work. After all, it is a stated purpose of school to prepare students to enter the workforce when their formal education is completed. And it is true that most school subjects are either directly or indirectly work-related. *Get a Job* asks teachers and students to figure out ways that the things being taught and learned in the world of school can be used in the world of work. Some of the connections are obvious. A class studying simple machines ought not to have too much trouble

finding applications of simple machines in the environment, whether construction site or kitchen. The built environment around us represents applications of geometry, architecture, health sciences, physical education, art, computer science, history, physics, music, and every other subject in the curriculum All school subjects have the potential to be linked to productive work of some kind.

PROCEDURE

One insightful middle school teacher I talked to told me that she had required of her seventh grade English students that they submit a poem, story, essay, or other writing to a journal for actual publication. When I asked her whether the students were discouraged by the rejection slips, she smiled and said that actually a couple submissions did, in fact, get published. But more than that, she went on, the kids learned that you have to follow certain conventions of style, punctuation, and so on, demanded by the journals and magazines. She felt that this was something about the real world worth learning. The publishing world is filled with career opportunities.

The entire built environment rests on ideas from science, art and architecture, mathematics, economics, culture, and so on. There is no scarcity of potential applications to be made. The very things that interest kids, including computers, cars, clothing, food, and a range of other technologies are inevitably linked by theory and application. The challenge should be to the students themselves to make the applications.

One variant of *Get a Job* is an extended role play, where each student assumes for a week that he/she has decided on some certain occupation, medicine, athletics, business, or design. The challenge for the students becomes that of documenting ways in which each assignment that they carry out is connected to their "career choice." It helps if students can interview someone, either in person or through written form, who actually is engaged in the particular career in order to obtain a realistic idea of just what skills, knowledge, and values are needed in order to do the work effectively.

OUTCOMES

For some students, the *Get a Job* strategy brings a concrete focus and sense of purpose to schoolwork that they had never considered. It may be just what some of your students need in order to get them take schoolwork seriously. The linkages between scholarly ideas and their applications in the world around us are very real. A problem for many students is that they don't know that. They need to be encouraged and required to go out and find the applications.

School-to-work programs are an excellent means of providing students with the insights they need to see the connection between what a builder does and what happens in a geometry class; what a person in advertising does and what happens in an English class; what a health science researcher does and what happens in a biology class. It has been estimated that there are in excess of 35,000 different occupations found in American society, and every one of them has some kind of linkage to the school curriculum.

EPILOGUE

> *The best part...is derived from reflection.*
> Samuel Taylor Coleridge

This is a book about practical ways to create a classroom environment where teaching, learning, and assessment come together to form a seamless whole. The vehicle for making this happen is *reflective practice*. Reflective practice has the power to change the way you and your students act, think, and feel about school life. This is because reflective practice asks more and gives more in return than business as usual. Reflective practice means not just doing things, covering the curriculum, carrying out assignments, and preparing for tests, but it means digging beneath the surface to unearth questions of purpose, meaning, value, and belonging.

Even in "better" classroom situations, reflective practice is the all-too-often missing ingredient, the factor that, if it *were* present, would make the difference between school as "that place you have to go to" and school as "that place you want to go to." Reflective practice is about caring, collaboration, integration, affiliation, and truth in teaching and learning.

When people are introduced to the strategies found in this text, they are initially of different opinions about whether they are, in fact, teaching, learning, or assessment strategies. My answer is invariably this: they are all three at once. They will change the way you and your students teach, the way you and your students learn, and the way you and your students assess hope, growth, and opportunity. And finally, these are small-scale activities, with a focus on life in classrooms and how that life might be improved.

I mentioned several times during the course of this book that the strategies are practical. Indeed they are, and in that spirit I make this promise: If you use them faithfully and consistently two things will happen. First, you and your students will notice achievement gains. I'm talking about real achievement, real learning. Standardized test scores should reflect these gains to a certain extent, but you will come to agree, I know you will, that the achievement gains you and your class realize are far greater than can be shown by such narrow measures of growth. Secondly, you and your students will come to know that the social/moral fabric of your school life has improved greatly. Standardized tests seldom take social and moral growth into account. This is a reminder that such tests have a purpose but that finally that purpose is rather limited.

Teaching is practical. Teaching is situated, that is, it happens at a particular time in a particular place with real people. Only those who have never been in the classroom would offer a different opinion. But excellent practice inevitably can be traced to theory. There are powerful ideas behind it. My experience with teachers and administrators, especially those who strive for excellence, is that they *do* care about where ideas come from. This is precisely why in Part One I drew your attention to the brief essays detailing the theoretical considerations that underlie the activities. Each of the essays was originally considerably longer. I distilled them to what I considered to be their essence. Those who wish to probe more deeply are invited to do so by investigating the references found at each chapter's end. This is what further inquiry is all about.

Part Two of the book was devoted to the activities themselves. Each activity in its own way is designed to help you and your students step back from whatever it is that you are doing and to reflect on the experience. These are *activities*, that is, they are things you do. Some of them call for writing, others for discussion, others for drawing, investigating, recording, record keeping, and other avenues that have potential for reflection. Each activity can be thought of as a lesson template. In other words, the activities use class time and homework in the same sense that other activities do. Some of the activities call for a higher teacher profile than others do. But all of them call upon students to be active, engaged, responsible, caring learners. In yet another sense, each of the activities is designed as an assessment procedure. You will find that you and your students are asking very basic questions about *what* is being learned, *how* it is being learned, and even *why* are we learning it.

Finally, I wish to say that the activities represent an academic quest as well as a social/moral quest. Academic, social, and moral growth represent the goal structure of the book. John Dewey, in his book *The School in Society*, noted that students bring four outstanding natural tendencies or instincts with them to school. These tendencies are at the heart of the academic, social, moral quest. The tendencies are: students' desire to converse, to construct, to inquire, and to express themselves.

You will have noticed that I reached back to Dewey's "natural tendencies" as the basis for the reflective activities. And as you continue to use the activities, you will find your students developing a conversational mode of learning, they will be making things and carrying out projects, they will be discovering and conducting inquiry, and they will be expressing themselves more openly, artistically, and authentically.

TAKE THIS TEST, *AGAIN!*

The following are a number of statements about teaching and learning. As you respond to them, you'll begin to get an idea of your own preliminary thoughts about some of the ideas contained in this book. When you have finished, just add up your numbers to get a score.

Mark "7" if you Strongly Agree; "3" if you are Not Sure; and "0" if you Strongly Disagree.

_____ School subjects should be taught in an integrated fashion.

_____ The student's role in learning should be active and initiatory.

_____ School learning should be primarily problem-focused.

_____ Students should play an active role in curriculum planning.

_____ Students should be given more time to discuss ideas with each other.

_____ Conversation, construction, and inquiry should receive major emphasis in the school day.

_____ Intrinsic motivation is the key to productive learning.

_____ Students should spend more time reflecting on ideas than mastering skills.

_____ Cooperative work and group projects should predominate.

_____ Students need class time to discuss the meaning and purpose of what they are learning.

_____ Students themselves ought to help decide what they should study.

_____ Student behavior and student interest are closely connected.

_____ The major purpose of assessment ought to be self-assessment.

_____ State and national standards will contribute little to real learning.

_____ Frontal, whole-class teaching should be kept to a minimum.

_____ Less time should be devoted to "covering" the curriculum.

Add up your score and compare it to the score you received when you took this same test at the beginning of this book. Any changes?

GLOSSARY

Affective domain

The area of education that focuses on the attitudinal/emotional development of students is often referred to as the affective domain. While this area may have always been a concern of educators to some degree, the more recent usage of the term was popularized by Benjamin Bloom in *Taxonomy of Educational Objectives* for the cognitive and affective domains, published respectively in 1956 and 1964. Bloom distinguished between learning that focuses on intellectual tasks, such as remembering or solving problems, and educational objectives that emphasize the affective nature of an individual such as interests, attitudes, and values. His work was based on the assumption that education must address the "whole person." In more recent years, the affective domain has been expanded to include a host of "whole person" areas, such as self-esteem, emotional and social adjustment, and political beliefs.

Assessment: authentic, alternative

An activity, instrument, or procedure designed to elicit what a person knows, feels, or can perform is referred to as an assessment. Assessment procedures typically used in schools range from the employment of standardized tests of achievement, preference, intelligence, adjustment, and so on, to classroom tests designed by publishers and teachers, to so-called authentic assessment procedures including self-assessment, portfolios, exhibitions, performances, journals, and so forth.

Basic skills

The term "basics" and "basic education" refer to those essentials in learning that every student should possess, or upon which many other subjects or areas of study depend.

Brain-based teaching

Brain-based teaching refers to those teaching approaches that are suggested by the theories derived from the basic research in brain functioning. The approaches generally require attention to hemisphericity, growth spurts, and modality. For example, a brain based teaching program might stress year-round schooling (growth spurts), integrated curriculum (hemisphericity), and verbal and visual explanations (modality). It is theorized that such educational approaches will result in greater learning because of how the brain is thought to function.

Child-centered, *see student-centered*

A child-centered approach to teaching and learning is one that shifts the center of gravity from the teacher to the student. An outcome of progressivism, child-centered education invokes the so-called doctrine of interest, which states basically that a child should be allowed to study whatever he/she wants to study, and that the teacher's role is to facilitate the child's interest. A child-centered environment is one in which students decide for themselves what they want to learn and how they want to learn it. Child-centered curricula generally favor exploratory learning, the arts, creativity, and the search for self-fulfillment over a predetermined scope and sequence of studies. The key to the child-centered curriculum is the growth and development of the individual. Meaningful learning results from individual exploration, investigation, and choosing what to learn. Believers in child-centered curriculum feel, that time spent in school learning someone else's knowledge, results in several serious deficiencies including lack of self-understanding, lack of interest, lack of meaning, and a general impression of school experience as lacking in relevance.

Cognitive domain

In Benjamin Bloom's *Taxonomy of Educational Objectives,* the area given over to memory and reasoning is that of the cognitive domain. One of the most important areas of psychology is devoted to the study of how humans learn to think, or the study of the cognitive domain. No unambiguous definition in psychological terms has yet emerged for the word "domain," or area of achievement, but it is believed to consist of four areas: cognitive, social, emotional, and physical. The cognitive domain was the first to be described by Benjamin Bloom in his taxonomy of learning objectives; the cognitive domain deals primarily with intellectual skills such as problem solving, memory, reasoning, comprehension, recall, and judgment. Compare to *affective domain.*

Concept mapping

A person's graphic, diagrammatic, or schematic representation of his or her understanding of a concept is referred to as a concept map. Construction of a concept map allows a learner to represent his/her level of knowledge of a concept in question while illustrating the concept's larger context in a web of related schematic knowledge. Thus, a map of the concept of "element" might illustrate not only its properties but its place in the context of atoms, molecules, other elements, and compounds.

Constructivism

Constructivism refers to a theory that learners construct their own knowledge and therefore their version of reality from their own unique experiences. It is this "construction" or schema that a learner then uses to accommodate and assimilate any new experience. The process of knowledge construction is thought to be an active one. Because of the complexities inherent in any real experience and because each learner's prior construction is unique, what someone learns in a given situation is often unpredictable.

In recent times, a difference of opinion has arisen between the so-called neo-Piagetian perspective, which emphasizes the individual's building of intellectual structures on the basis of his/her experiences, and the so-called neo-Vygotskyian perspective, which emphasizes the sociocultural melieu in which learning experiences take place. The differences are profound enough to have touched off considerable debate within the constructivist movement. Nevertheless, both perspectives take into account the idea that knowledge is socially constructed by human beings as opposed to being composed of preexistent entities that learners are merely "taught."

Constructivist approach, *see also Cognitive Domain, Discovery learning*

Constructivism is a model of cognition that emphasizes the active construction, testing, and reconstruction of cognitive models of the student's world. It is based on the belief that the cognitive development of a child is due to a continuous process of construction and reconstruction of the child's sense of reality. Persons or groups constitute or construct reality; behind the form or thing there exists a process which creates it, or which leads to its coming into being. The constructivist approach owes much to Gestalt perception psychology which contends that there is a myriad of interpretations to the same "picture" or event, and that people actively organize their worlds into meaningful wholes. In the educational psychology, constructivism has its roots in a number of paradigms, including those of Piaget, Dewey, Vygotsky, and Montessori. In psychology, constructivism is an axiom of existential, phenomenological, Gestalt, Piagetian, Vygotskyian, perception theorist, and cognitive science approaches. More recent contributors to the constructivist movement include Paul Cobb, D.C. Phillips, Nell Noddings, and E. Von Glasersfeld. Critics include Carl Bereiter and M.R. Matthews

In its school-based applications, the constructivist approach encourages an active, creative process in the student. It is more concerned with understandings achieved through relevant experience and activity than with accumulated facts received from others; more imbued with meaning; more domain or situation specific; more influenced by social and cultural contexts; and, in general, less purely cognitive and less governed by abstract principles than traditional conceptions of learning.

A common critical contention is that constructivism suffers from an identity crisis. It has variously been called a rehash of the Socratic method, warmed-over John Dewey, discovery learning revisited, the activity curriculum one more time, and new, improved Piaget. There are many different views of constructivism and no assurance whether the different views will or should coalesce into a coherent theoretical model.

Another criticism questions whether the academic content of a course will suffer in order to use the process involved in a constructivist classroom. By emphasizing process, content may suffer. The relationship of academic content knowledge and the use of constructivism remains an unresolved issue.

Cooperative learning

Cooperative learning is an approach to the teaching/learning process, which has been proposed as a viable alternative to the current individualistic and competitive practices of schools. There are several forms of cooperative learning, but they all involve students working in groups or teams to achieve certain educational goals. Some proponents propose it as a generic strategy that could be used in any setting, while others have designed subject-matter specific strategies. The research claims that detail the elements of cooperative learning are as elaborate and documented as those of any other movement in education today.

Cooperative learning involves students working in groups or teams to achieve certain mutually agreed upon learning goals. Beyond the most basic premise of working together, students must also depend on each other, a concept called *positive interdependence*.

Creativity

Creativity is associated with such terms as originality, imaginative thought, problem solving, and artistry. Creativity is linked to notions of excellence and original contributions in music, the arts, and so on. From a teaching/learning standpoint, creativity seems to fluorish in more open, tolerant environments where necessary help is provided by expert teachers. High level creativity requires extensive knowledge, flexibility, and the continual reorganization of ideas. Because any efforts at creative production involve risk taking by the creator, a supportive, appreciative environment seems crucial.

Critical thinking

Although no proof exists that one type of thinking is of a higher order than another, there is a general consensus among educators that thinking and activities that include analysis, synthesis, judgement, evaluation, reflection, and so on, are more intellectually stimulating than memory work or even attempts to comprehend. Most hierarchies, including Benjamin Bloom's, assume that one cannot think and act productively at "higher levels" without basic information and knowledge.

Various terms are used for critical thinking including, higher order thinking skills, problem solving skills, strategic reasoning skills, productive thinking skills, and so on.

Discovery learning

This teaching/learning approach is based on inductive thinking and was popularized in the 1960s by the cognitive psychologist Jerome Bruner and others. In discovery learning, students work on their own to discover basic principles. It involves asking questions, exploration, data gathering, concluding, and generalizing. Advocates of discovery learning generally point to the process of acquiring knowledge as coequal with the product or answer itself. It is their contention that students must experience the process of how knowledge is created in order to better understand information, ideas, and skills.

Divergent thinking

Divergent thinking refers to a process where learners are encouraged to derive multiple solutions or differing solutions to problems. Often associated with creativity, divergent thinking involves originality, fluency, and flexibility. Divergent answers or solutions are generally more stimulus-free than conventional answers and are associated with insight, new applications, paradigm shifts, and a wide range of possibilities. Divergent thinking processes include invention, creativity, artistry, brainstorming, use of metaphor, problem solving, and critical thinking. Divergent thinking is sometimes identified with the lateral thinking discussed by Edward deBono who refers to those moments when we make the unexpected move or connection, as a result of deviation from a course or standard.

Effective schooling

Effective schooling research is an area of educational research that focuses on schools and classrooms with similar populations that are classified as effective and ineffective, and then notes differences in their organization, management, curriculum, and instruction.

Goal structure

Goal structure refers to the way in which students relate to others who are also working toward a certain goal. Used, in particular, by advocates of *cooperative learning*, the term is most often invoked to differentiate among cooperative goal structures where students work together toward a common goal; individualistic goal structures where a common goal may be understood but where people work alone to achieve it; and competitive goal structures where learners work as rivals or as defacto rivals to attain a certain goal.

Hierarchy of needs

Commonly known as Maslow's hierarchy, this construct by the psychologist Abraham Maslow suggests that all humans needs can be subsumed into two major categories, each with levels, deficiency needs and being needs. Deficiency needs are, in ascending order: physiological, safety, belongingness and love, and esteem needs. Being needs include: the need to know and understand, aesthetic needs, and self-actualization needs. Maslow was convinced that these needs are hierarchical in nature and that any given level of needs can be met only if those needs subsumed below it are first met.

Individual differences

The concept of individual differences implies that no two given individuals are alike with respect to *motivation*, knowledge, aptitude, *interest*, ability, and other variables related to learning. This key pedagogical idea is the basis for such alternative strategies as continuous progress, individualized instruction, child-centered programs, elective courses, and other innovations which have been implemented from time to time in opposition to such traditional school features as whole-class instruction, annual promotions, age-related grade placement, seat-time, common assignments, and so on.

Inquiry learning

Inquiry learning is a teaching/learning approach in which students use systematized problem-solving procedures to find answers to questions. Questions are often those that are of interest to learners and/or based on their needs, but inquiry can also be used in more structured, academic settings as well, where students are learning formal subject matter. In a foundational sense, inquiry learning is based on the classic conception of inductive reasoning formulated by Francis Bacon. In inquiry, as in induction, one reasons from particulars toward an inference or generalization, always using empirical methods.

Instructional conversation

Instruction, or the guiding of learning in more or less formal settings, is generally classified either as direct instruction or as non-directive teaching. The former is teacher-centered and the latter is learner-centered. Direct instruction proceeds with frontal teaching utilizing lecture, class discussion, teacher demonstrations and explanations. Direct instruction is usually script-dependent in that it proceeds on the basis of objectives external to the student, teaching of skills, content, and so on, and culminating in tests of mastery. Non-directive teaching is more commonly associated with such approaches as interest centers, *discovery learning*, problem-solving, *cooperative learning*, project learning, and so on.

Interest

The term interest is often used by developmentalists to mean an approach to the curriculum whereby the learner makes decisions about what to study based on what he/she is interested in. Purists are careful to point out that interest should not be confused with curiosity or other superficial inclinations. In an interest-based approach to learning, it is incumbent upon the teacher to study students and to know them well in order to support their learning interests. But ultimately, the student's innate desire to learn is the key to growth and development.

Learning styles, *see Modality of teaching*

Learning styles represent the consistent pattern of behaviors that can be associated with each individual as he/she approaches, interprets, and acts on a learning experience. The basic research of this area is found in brain research and personality types. A number of models of learning styles have been proposed by individuals such as Rita and Kenneth Dunn, Marie Carbo, and Herman Witkin.

Literacy

Literacy is generally meant to describe a level of reading, writing, and communication abilities that permit an individual to learn through print modalities as well as through electronic means.

Locus of control

Locus of control is the "place" where a person locates the source of responsibility for his/her successes and failures. The concept was originally developed by the psychologist J.B. Rotter. Rotter felt that locus of control is a fairly stable construct which essentially differentiates self-determination from control by others. People who have an internal locus of control believe they are largely responsible for their own fate, while those who have an external locus of control assume that circumstances beyond their own effort, initiative, and so on, account for the outcomes in their lives. An internal locus of control is often associated with higher *self-esteem,* and an external locus of control with lower self-esteem.

Mastery learning

The term "mastery" was introduced by Benjamin Bloom as a means of identifying when a student had learned a certain skill or content. Because of the ambiguities involved in what it means for someone to have "learned" something, a criterion measure, usually 80% correct, is often invoked. The term is perhaps as misleading as it is useful, because anyone knows that a learner who has completed a worksheet or activity has probably not mastered the material in the common sense of the word.

Meaning-centered, meaning-driven

A meaning-centered approach is an approach to learning, which seeks relevance and avoids isolated skills as means of achieving *literacy*. Meaning-centered instruction focuses on building knowledge and understanding within the natural framework of a child's experience, an important concept with the whole-language educational philosophy.

Metacognition

Metacognition is a theory which states that learners benefit by thoughtfully and reflectively considering the things they are learning and the ways in which they are learning them. A common phrase used by its advocates is "thinking about thinking." In classroom situations, metacognition could well involve "thinking aloud" with a partner, so that each participant gains insight to the processes that lead to intellectual conclusions. Carried to further levels, metacognition might involve reflective thinking by students about the value and/or the applicability of the things they are learning.

Modality teaching

Modality teaching refers to the practice of using a variety of strategies, activities, explanations, and so on, for the same content. Learning modalities are said to be sensory channels through which individuals give, receive, and store information. On the basis of brain research and learning styles research, students are thought to be visual, auditory, tactile-kinesthetic, or mixed modality learners. Modality teaching offers a variety of instructional approaches to reach the different types of learners. For example, modality teaching in arithmetic uses verbal explanations, written examples on the chalkboard or on a handout, and manipulative hands-on math materials for the students which correspond to the task to be learned.

Moral development

Moral development refers to a theory or set of theories, which postulates that individuals pass through various and predetermined stages of moral reasoning. Most notable of the theorists is Lawrence Kohlberg. His theories were very influential during the 1960s and 1970s and resulted in a number of books, courses, and materials for teacher training in moral education and a wide number of moral education programs for children. These programs usually employed *moral dilemmas* as teaching techniques based on the belief that such intellectual discussions would raise the level of moral reasoning.

However, researchers in the area were never able to demonstrate that changes in moral reasoning actually changed a person's behavior.

Motivation

Motivation can be defined as those factors within a person that arouse and direct goal-oriented behavior. Teachers are interested in why some students are motivated to learn certain things, just how deeply motivated or how serious they are, and why some students persevere while others become discouraged and give up on a task. It is useful to distinguish between what is called intrinsic motivation or the pursuit of certain activities for their own reward, and extrinsic motivation, or the pursuit of activities in response to such factors as rewards and punishments. However, it is not easy to untangle the two.

Multiple intelligences

Howard Gardner's theory of multiple intelligences attempts to broaden our definition of human intelligence. The theory deals with capacities or skills that are found universally in humans, although multiple intelligences theory recognizes that individual culture affects the manifestations of problem-solving skills in a given society. Because it is neurally based, each intelligence comes into play as a result of internally and externally presented information

Paradigm

The terms *paradigm* and *paradigm shift* were popularized by Thomas Kuhn is his book, *The Structure of Scientific Revolutions*. In that book Kuhn suggested that our worldview, whether scientific or not, is conditioned by a prevailing paradigm or model. He suggested further that scientific knowledge advances not incrementally as is generally supposed but on the basis of paradigm shifts or new fundamental insights that allow completely different ways of thinking about things.

Psychosocial development

Some psychologists and educators believe that individuals pass through specific stages of development on their way to maturity. These are referred to as developmental stages. Developmental stages have been theorized in a number of areas, but the most common theories revolve around the cognitive, moral, and psychosocial domains. For example, Jean Piaget theorized that children's thinking, or cognitive development, progressed through four stages, each qualitatively different from the previous stage: sensorimotor (0-2 years), preoperational (2-7 years), concrete operational (7-11 years), and formal operational (11-16 years). Lawrence Kohlberg postulated that individuals pass through various and predetermined stages of moral reasoning (*moral development*) which he called preconventional, conventional, and postconventional morality. Erik Erikson theorized that psychosocial development is, or can be, a life-long process involving eight sequential stages, each with a task to be accomplished by the individual before he/she can move on to the next stage. These and other theories of development have implications for educators in the areas of "developmentally appropriate" curricula, teaching strategies, and educational goals, and many have greatly influenced education in these areas at one time or another.

Pedagogics

Pedagogics is a term used more frequently in Europe than in the United States to identify the practice of education involving curriculum, *teaching, a*nd *learning.*

Reciprocal teaching

Reciprocal teaching is a technique for improving students' reading comprehension. It involves a four-step group teaching/learning process in which students (1) summarize the contents of a passage, (2) ask questions about the main idea of the passage, (3) clarify the difficult aspects of the material, and (4) predict what will happen next. Generally, reciprocal teaching begins as a teacher-centered strategy with the teacher modeling the steps, but the idea is for the center of gravity to shift to the students, creating a peer teaching effect.

Reflective thinking

Reflective thinking is an approach used in teaching in which a problem (in teaching or learning) is first set or interpreted in theory, experiences, and understandings, and then a solution to the problem is developed through testing, self-evaluations, and a series of revisions. It is inquiry-oriented, and, as the title suggests, it is reflective, in that learners are expected to take the measure of their experience, to consider it thoughtfully, and to reach conclusions about the worth or efficacy of the approach they took. Often reflective thinking is encouraged in environments where students compare their problem-solving processes with each other, with those of an expert, or with an ideal model. The origins of reflective thinking as a teaching and learning strategy are found in the works of John Dewey.

Schema theory

Schema theory refers to a concept that focuses on the relationship between prior knowledge and comprehension. The theory explains the way in which experiences and related concepts are stored in memory. Schema (schemata, *pl.*) is the individual's internal explanation of the nature of situations, objects, and so on, that are encountered; it is the way knowledge is organized within the brain. These schemata are constantly being altered and/or changed as new knowledge is absorbed.

Seatwork

Seatwork, or working at one's desk alone, is among the most common events in school life. Seatwork is often assigned following a lesson in which the teacher has explained certain skills, ideas, procedures, and so on. John Goodlad reported in his book, *A Study of Schooling*, that seatwork is the single most predictable occurrence in the lives of elementary school children. Seatwork usually involves workbooks, dittoes, worksheets, textbooks, and exercises. There is general consensus among researchers that seatwork is greatly overused in our schools.

Self-esteem, *see Locus of control*

Self-esteem involves the estimation individuals place on their own perceived attributes, capacities, intentions, and behaviors. The related term, "self-concept," is used interchangeably referring to the aggregate of perceptions, ideas, feelings, and attitudes an individual has about him/herself. Considerable controversy exists over whether self-esteem contributes to achievement or achievement contributes to self-esteem, or whether self-esteem is even a stable enough construct to be accorded a sense of validity.

Strategies

In school settings, strategies are general, long-term procedures used to accomplish certain stated goals. Strategic planning takes into account underlying purposes and cumulative effects over time. Tactics are methods by which *strategies* are implemented. Tactics have a day-to-day aspect and are the kinds of maneuvers good teachers make in order to keep students engaged, focused, and achievement-oriented. Teaching strategies are the approaches or methods teachers use in order to ensure student *learning*. Broadly speaking, teaching strategies can be broken down into two large categories: direct and indirect instruction. Direct instruction tends to be teacher-centered and is exemplified by lecture, class discussion, and related means of whole-class instruction. Indirect strategies tend to shift the center of gravity to the student. Examples of indirect instruction include *cooperative learning*, project methods, *discovery learning*, and learning centers.

Taxonomy of educational objectives

The Taxonomy of Educational Objectives, Cognitive Domain, a hierarchical, six-level construct of intellectual activity, was published by Benjamin Bloom in 1956. Its influence in educational circles has been enormous, and practically every educational text and teacher training program for the past three decades has included it as fundamental to thinking about curricular and instructional activities. Bloom and his colleagues also developed known taxonomies for both the *affective* and psychomotor domains, but these efforts have had far less influence. Bloom's construct of intellectual activity begins at the lower end with memory work involving bits and pieces of information and culminates at the top end with evaluation or judgment. In spite of its pervasive influence, no actual proof exists that the intellectual hierarchy Bloom constructed is ultimately real.

Teaching

Jean Piaget described teaching as the establishing of environments where students' cognitive structures could emerge and grow. Such a description would match the conception of the teacher as facilitator. An advocate of *direct instruction* might describe teaching as the act of imparting needed skills, knowledge, and values to learners. But those who hold to either perspective would agree that teaching involves far more than child-minding. Teaching includes planning, organizing, reflecting, acting, reacting, assessing, and above all, continuous problem solving.

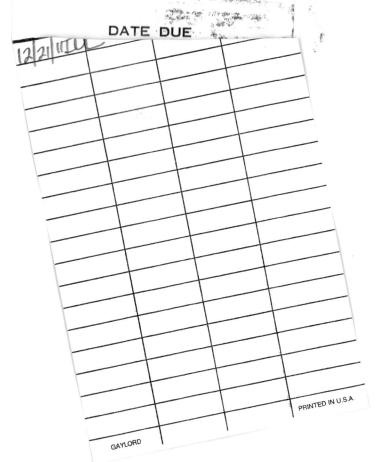

DATE DUE

12/21/11

GAYLORD   PRINTED IN U.S.A.